YORK NOTES

General Editors: Professor A.N. Jeffares (*University of Stirling*) & Professor Suheil Bushrui (*American University of Beirut*)

Mark Twain

TOM SAWYER

Notes by Mary Ross

BA PH D (STIRLING) DIPED (DUNDEE)
Tutor in charge of English, Newbattle Abbey College

 LONGMAN
YORK PRESS

YORK PRESS
Immeuble Esseily, Place Riad Solh, Beirut.

LONGMAN GROUP LIMITED
London
Associated companies, branches and representatives
throughout the world

© Librairie du Liban 1980

First published 1980
ISBN 0 582 78125 6
Printed in Hong Kong by
Wing Tai Cheung Printing Co Ltd

Contents

Part 1: Introduction   *page* 5
  A note on the text   13

Part 2: Summaries   14
  A general summary   14
  Detailed summaries   15

Part 3: Commentary   45
  The basic plan   48
  Language and style   49
  Perspective   53
  Tom and literature   58
  Tom and America   59
  The characters   60
  Major points from the commentary   64

Part 4: Hints for study   67
  Points for special study   67
  Suitable quotations   70
  Language   73
  Sample questions and answers   75

Part 5: Suggestions for further reading   88

The author of these notes   90

Part 1

Introduction

Samuel Langhorne Clemens (Mark Twain) was born in Florida, Missouri, on 30 November 1835. His father was a man who, although he tried many occupations, seemed to be dogged by ill fortune. At a time when the country was expanding and fortunes were being made on every side, John Marshall Clemens remained a hard-working failure, constantly moving his family further and further westwards in pursuit of success. When Samuel Clemens was born, his father was the owner of a store but, threatened by bankruptcy, he left Florida in 1839 and settled in a town thirty miles away, a town called Hannibal. It was here, on the banks of the great Mississippi River, that Twain grew up, watching the steamboats coming and going, absorbing the atmosphere of a place whose population expanded at an almost incredible rate.

In 1830, there were thirty people in the place; by 1847, there were two thousand five hundred. Hannibal's tremendous rate of growth was related to its position on the river. The surge of people into the unexploited lands of the West meant that Hannibal grew rapidly as an important landing place for the supplies needed by these pioneers.

What life in Hannibal was like for a child is reflected in Twain's writings, especially in *The Adventures of Tom Sawyer* (1876) and its sequel, *The Adventures of Huckleberry Finn* (1884). However, Twain's attitude to the place where he grew up is not a simple one. St Petersburg, the name he gives Hannibal in *Tom Sawyer*, is not without its faults, faults which stem from the attitude of its inhabitants. In *Huckleberry Finn*, these faults emerge even more clearly and it is plain that Twain, in this book, is deeply troubled by the way in which his countrymen are responding to the tremendous opportunities offered them by the new land. He, like other American writers, saw that man was fraught with greed, with hypocrisy and with selfishness, flaws which, in the relatively bare landscapes of such early settlements as Hannibal, stood out even more clearly than they did in the cities of the eastern part of the United States and which did not bode well for the future of the South-West.

Twain's pessimism about mankind was not, of course, a thing of his youth. When his father died in 1847, leaving the family in extreme poverty, Twain left school and became a printer's apprentice, a trade which his elder brother, Orion, had taken up ten years before. In 1849 Orion returned to Hannibal and bought up the two local papers. Twain worked with him until, in 1853, it was clear that Orion was as bad a businessman as his father had been. Twain, now master of a trade which ensured that he could get a job wherever there was a newspaper, moved east to St Louis, New York and Philadelphia. Then, hearing that there were fortunes to be made in South America, he began his journey south again, arriving in New Orleans in 1857. Here he discovered that there were no boats going to South America, so instead he decided to train as a pilot on the steamboats.

At this point, Twain was only twenty-one years old and there is little doubt that he still regarded the steamboats, which had been the sole source of excitement in the Hannibal of his early youth, in a romantic light. By 1859 he had fulfilled a boyhood dream by becoming a fully qualified sea pilot. His experiences on the river are recounted in *Life on the Mississippi* (1883), a book which is an expanded version of the story 'Old Times on the Mississippi' which he wrote in 1875. It is from this period of his life that Twain derived his pen-name. The pilots, sounding the depth of water below the steamboats, would shout out, 'Mark one,' 'Mark twain,' 'Mark three,' and so on, to indicate the number of fathoms below the boat.

In 1861, the war between the Northern and Southern States broke out. This, the American Civil War, was centred on the issue of slavery. Most of the Southern States, including Missouri, were so-called 'slave states', employing Negro labour and regarding Negroes as if they were marketable goods rather than people. The non-slave states of the North deplored this inhumane practice and, in 1861, brought the issue to a head with a declaration of war. Twain's feelings about the issue were mixed. He himself came from a slave-owning family and had been brought up to believe that slavery was a natural state of affairs. However, as a man of increasing humane concern, he was already questioning these assumptions. He left the river at the outbreak of war and went back to Hannibal, where he briefly joined an almost comically ill-organised group of slave-owning gentlemen called the Marion Rangers. After a fortnight of wandering about uncertainly the Rangers broke up and Twain, with his brother Orion, headed west to Nevada where Orion had obtained the post of secretary to the governor. The journey, into new, exciting territory, was later to form the subject of Twain's book, *Roughing It* (1872).

On arriving in Nevada, Twain soon heard that people were finding silver in large quantities two hundred miles away in Humboldt. He immediately set off but proved to be unlucky as a 'prospector' (a man who bought land in the hope that he would find gold or silver ore on it), in spite of much strenuous effort and the expenditure of a large amount of money on pieces of likely-looking land. It was at this time that he witnessed human greed at its worst, the image of men striving and killing in the pursuit of wealth. Under the impact of such an image, it is highly probable that Twain's youthful optimism about mankind began to be modified. He returned to Virginia City to work as a journalist and, in 1863, wrote his first humorous piece under the pen-name of Mark Twain. In 1865, the publication of a short piece entitled 'Jim Smiley and his Jumping Frog', first in a New York paper and then in papers all over the United States, established Twain's reputation as a humorist. He was commissioned to go to the Sandwich Islands, from whence he sent back many humorous letters and on which he delivered his first public lecture in 1866. Public lectures were extremely popular in America at this time, and Twain proved to have great abilities as a public speaker.

For a long time after 1865, Twain enjoyed unbroken success, both as a writer and as a public speaker. In 1867 he went on a tour of the Holy Land as correspondent for a newspaper. From this journey he drew the material for the novel which made his reputation once and for all, *The Innocents Abroad* (1869). This was a collection of the letters he had written on the voyage for the benefit of American newspaper readers. Throughout the novel, the tone is consistently humorous, at the expense of the narrator himself and his fellow-passengers, and of the sights and sounds which the Old World offered to the tourist. Twain voiced all the feelings which must have been suppressed by many of the Americans who went to Europe and beyond in search of culture, and who felt too intimidated by the older culture to dare to say that they either did not like it or found it boring. It is, of course, likely that Mark Twain deliberately exaggerated the ignorance of the narrator of the book to produce a comic effect. But that narrator, Mark Twain, was taken to the hearts of Americans, who no doubt felt that in him they had found a champion, someone who voiced criticisms of the Old World and did so with vigour, with humour and without embarrassment. The book's popularity may be judged by the fact that, within the first year of its publication, sixty thousand copies were sold.

In 1870, Twain married a girl called Olivia Langdon, whom he had loved since first meeting her in 1867. He had undertaken to write another book to follow the successful *Innocents Abroad*, but found himself bedevilled by personal and business problems. However, by 1872 he had purchased a large house, finished the book, *Roughing It*, and was embarked on another lecture tour to pay off his debts. It was at this point, too, that he started to indulge in what was to become a life-long preoccupation, inventing things. Only one of these inventions ever worked. The remainder merely cost Twain time and money, sometimes bringing him near to bankruptcy.

This same year Twain went to England, primarily to meet other writers but also to collect material for another book. He met many writers, including Lewis Carroll (Charles Dodgson, 1832-98) and the Russian Ivan Turgenev (1818-83), but he never produced the book. The relationship between America and Britain is, of course, a unique one in that, up to a certain point, they share the same history and then they divide radically. Nonetheless Twain liked England and was well received there, and this, perhaps, is why he did not subject England to any destructive humour.

His attitude to the history of England is interesting. In *Tom Sawyer*, we see Tom and Joe recreating the exploits of the popular English folk-hero, Robin Hood, and hear Tom reflecting that he would rather be Robin Hood for one day than President of the United States for ever. Robin Hood, of course, as a social outcast with right on his side, appeals to the child Tom, possessing many of the qualities most admired by the boy. But when we see Huck, in *Huckleberry Finn*, recounting the history of English kings to Jim, his Negro friend, and making them out to be an unbroken line of woman-beheading tyrants, then we discern a curious attitude on the part of the author himself. The figures of English history are romantic, yet they are also appalling to one born under a democratic system. Only the outcast who fights (like Robin Hood) for the underdog, the poor or powerless human being, gains unqualified approval. As a writer, Twain felt the need for historical and mythical figures and America would not, at this point in its history, supply them. It was, therefore, natural that Twain should turn to England as a source of such figures, for its history was also, up to a point, the history of his own country. He made two attempts to deal more directly with this history, in *The Prince and the Pauper* (1881) and *A Connecticut Yankee* (1889). In the latter, he tries to use history to show how far man is a creature of his heredity and his environment, dropping a figure from nineteenth-century America into the midst of sixth-century England.

By 1893, Twain's disillusionment with mankind in general, and America in particular, was becoming very evident in his writings. In 1876, Hannibal was the St Petersburg of *Tom Sawyer*; in 1884, it was still St Petersburg, but the corruption and hypocrisy, the cruelty and the inhumanity of slavery, were beginning to be very obvious; by 1893 Hannibal had become Dawson's Landing in *Pudd'nhead Wilson*, a book which is an outright condemnation of, amongst other things, slavery. The basic story, of a part-Negro child secretly substituted for the child of the white slave-owner and so brought up believing in white superiority, is unmistakable in its import. When the boy grows up and discovers the truth, he sells his own mother to another slave-owner, thus proving the brutality and irrationality of the whole system. By the time Hannibal has become Hadleyburg in 'The Man That Corrupted Hadleyburg' (1899), it no longer bears any resemblance to the St Petersburg of *Tom Sawyer*. Money, as Twain had seen in Nevada, is a corrupting force and within the setting of a small town, the corruption can be made to appear even more appalling.

Towards the end of his career, Twain was heavily in debt, on account of the failure of publishing companies in which he was involved and of the failure of his biggest, costliest invention, a type of printing press. This meant that he was forced to embark on more lecture tours and to write books and stories whose quality was far below that of earlier works. The pessimism and disillusion now apparent in his writings and also in his lectures did not, however, seriously affect his popularity. As he became a crusader against slavery, against corruption and even against certain European regimes, his readers followed him with a blind devotion which left them convinced that he was a humorist.

It is apparent, even from this brief sketch, that Twain lived an enormously varied life, that he was quick to seize on any experience and was adept at translating that experience into literature. He was, of course, fortunate in so far as he was living at a time of enormous change and expansion within America itself. He witnessed and partook in the last great push westwards, the quest of the dispossessed people from Europe for a place in the world. The frontier, that line between the civilised and the untamed lands, has been an important factor in shaping the American outlook. It is now a myth, one of the yardsticks against which modern man may measure himself. The frontier, and the people who pushed it back, are seen in countless American novels to possess certain desirable qualities. The untamed land, in its natural state, is seen as a model for man, something which reflects his real nature, something unspoiled by the overlay of civilisation. It is, in a sense, the American Garden of Eden, the place of primal innocence and virtue. The people who go out to challenge and tame this wilderness somehow partake of its qualities. Being close to nature, they are ennobled. In real terms, the pushing back of the frontier demanded immense stamina and devotion. Those who did it were for the most part desperate people, without any hope of a reasonable existence anywhere save in the wilderness which they must tame.

These generalisations about the role of the frontier in American literature apply to both *Tom Sawyer* and *Huckleberry Finn*. As children, Tom and Huck are both in a state of innocence. The world for them is a place to be explored, full of excitement, of promise and of the unknown. The streets, the houses and the church in St Petersburg are not their natural home. The boys are much happier when they are out of doors, in the woods, covered in natural dirt rather than unnaturally clean. They take an intense interest in the minute things of nature, the bugs, rats and cats which the civilised adults take pains to exclude from their homes. Tom and his friends do not run their lives according to the rules of the Christian religion but according to superstitions which always hinge on some natural phenomenon. They do not deal in money, but use the much more primitive and direct method of barter, exchanging goods directly for goods. Thus they are, in every sense, much nearer to the spirit of the frontier than any of the adult characters in the books.

In using children, Twain was working within a venerable tradition, the tradition of the child as the 'noble savage' (the untamed human animal with an inborn dignity and an instinctive sense of right and wrong). It is for this reason, amongst others, that both *Tom Sawyer* and *Huckleberry Finn* cannot simply be dismissed as children's books. Certainly, they are books which appeal to children, for children love to read of people with whom they can identify.

But if the books are capable of gripping the imagination of children, they are also capable of diverting the intellect of the adult, for they work most successfully on the two levels. They are both adventure stories and profound comments on the state of American society. Tom is young and has to learn many things, such as the difference between right and wrong; the young nation has, like Tom, to learn many lessons and to find its own identity. Both are innocent; both may be shaped according to their experience of the world. They hang in the balance between good and evil, between corruption and continued virtue. As Twain makes clear, virtue does not reside in the sort of morality preached by Mr Sprague, but in the kind of action taken by Huck and Tom and in their courageous honesty.

However, having said that Huck and Tom and their fellows are far more at home in the natural environment than in the civilised setting of the town, it is clear that when Tom, Joe and Huck go to Jackson's Island, they are thoroughly frightened and wish nothing more than the comfort of an ordered and sheltered life. This is not so contradictory as it might first appear. Twain does not suggest to us that we should live in a totally primitive state. This is impractical and, as the terror of the children when they are left alone shows, exaggerated. Twain's desire is for a compromise rather better than the one which is being effected in St Petersburg itself. The town, perched on the edge of the wilderness, tries to maintain all the trappings of civilised life. Not all these trappings are bad. A certain measure of shelter from the elements, of mutual support and comfort, are desirable. What is undesirable is the complete abandonment of all real contact with nature and with natural things. A loss of contact is much more obvious in *Huckleberry Finn*, where there is a constant juggling between appearance and reality, with all the jugglers save Huck and Jim being intent on personal gain. Huck and Jim, floating down the great river on a raft, are emblematic of true freedom, of what man can be when left to his own devices and in direct contact with nature. Racial issues are resolved on the raft, moral problems dealt with in a humane way, whilst, on either side of the river, we see corruption, degradation and greed creating unhappiness and a loss of moral worth in those who live there.

Having sketched the life of Mark Twain and having indicated briefly the larger issues with which *Tom Sawyer* deals, we must place Twain in the context of other American writers of his time. As the sketch of his life has shown, he was a highly individualistic character, in the later stages of his life openly turning against the direction in which American society was moving and publicly condemning it. In spite of this individuality, however, Twain was influenced in his writing by his contemporaries such as Johnson J. Hooper (1815-62), Artemus Ward (Charles Farrar Browne, 1834-67), James W. Riley (1849-1916) and William Dean Howells (1837-1920), and by considerations of what the public wanted to read. In all his early works he adopted the pose of a humorous narrator, sometimes naïve to the point of being ignorant, as in *The Innocents Abroad*, in others merely an observer with an eye for the humorous potential of any given scene. Twain's choice of the humorous vein was not simply a reflection of his own humorous personality but a reflection of the cultural context from which he came and of the fact that humorists were popular with the reading public of the day.

That cultural context is difficult to imagine or describe and virtually impossible to define. The Southern States of America have an identity of their own, an identity which was no doubt finally forged when they came together in 1861 to resist the attack from the North and which, after the overthrow of this resistance, lingered on as a nostalgia for the gracious and ordered days when society was arranged in a neat hierarchy, white landowners at the top, slaves at the bottom. It is this nostalgia which, when mixed with an awareness of the fundamental inhumanity of the arrangement, has given inspiration to such distinguished writers as William Faulkner (1897-1962) and John Steinbeck (1902-68) and to such lesser, but nevertheless worthwhile, writers as Sherwood Anderson (1876-1941) and Carson McCullers (1917-67). In other words, the region from which Twain came had a distinct identity. And that identity proved fruitful soil for the growth of the imagination.

Perhaps the best way to attempt to understand the culture of the Southern States is to look at their history. America was, of course, colonised largely by the English in the seventeenth century. The colonists, who had gone to America for a variety of reasons, many of them not very creditable, became extremely defensive about their new home, especially as those in the 'mother country' tended to regard them as something of a joke. At first the colonists tried to reply to the jokes by exaggerated insistence on how wonderful it was to be in America, how rich the land was and how refined life was. Those who responded most often to the criticisms from England were the inhabitants of Virginia, in the South. Seeing that in England, the sophisticated élite were being amused by the cultivated wit of the essayists and critics Joseph Addison (1672-1719) and **Richard Steele** (1672-1729), the late eighteenth-century Virginians began to copy the humorous model. At first they also copied the refined and artificial tone as well as the humour, but gradually, with the expansion of the frontier and the greater experience of real hardship, such gentility began to wane. Instead there grew up a tradition of telling exaggerated stories about the frontier, of openly inviting the world to laugh not with the Southern American but at him, then proving, in the end, that he had a certain native cunning which made him superior to those who mocked him. It was this tradition which was available to Twain when he started writing and it was this tradition which he adopted and refined to its highest point.

By 1815, according to one observer, the inhabitants of the South had developed a language and a manner of pronouncing words which were unique to them and which were quite distinct from English as spoken in England. This language, born out of and therefore reflecting the world of the South, was recreated in all its many subtle variations by Twain and became an added weapon in his battery of humorous tools. Indeed, he is generally recognised as having introduced the vernacular, or native speech, to Southern literature, and having done so superbly. At the outset of *Huckleberry Finn*, Twain lists and comments on the number of dialects that he uses in the book. They are 'the Missouri Negro dialect; the extremist form of the backwoods Southwestern dialect; the ordinary "Pike County" dialect; and four modified varieties of this last.' These varieties have been, Twain assures us, 'done painstakingly' and, indeed, he had an excellent ear for the variations in dialect and tone. In *Tom Sawyer* the variations are fewer but we see, in the way in which the words are spelt, an attempt to recreate the sound of the words as they would be spoken by the characters.

These variations in dialect reflected, of course, the differing social positions of the speakers. Twain's South was a place of very marked social degrees. The slaves, who were undoubtedly regarded by many of the whites as being less than human, spoke in a very thick dialect, running words together and shortening them at the ends even more than the white population. Amongst the whites, the lowest rank were the so-called 'poor whites' who scraped a bare living from poor soil or were, like Huck's father and Muff Potter, social outcasts. The upper-middle class consisted of the plantation owners, who, with all their work being done for them by slaves, had the leisure to indulge in literary pursuits and to copy the ways of the gentry in England. Their speech, their manners and their customs were the most leisurely and refined of all.

Thus Mark Twain emerged from a fairly complex cultural context and took his place within an existing literary tradition, that of humorous writing. From the publication of *Huckleberry Finn* till his death in 1910, however, he gradually turned his humour against the very people for whom he wrote. The discovery of some unpublished works after Twain's death revealed, as never before, the extent to which the humorist had become an embittered cynic, a man disillusioned by what was happening around him and doubtful about the possibilities for the future. Gone were the innocence and joy found in *Tom Sawyer*; in their place stood greed, hypocrisy and an increasing dissatisfaction with a world which had once promised so much.

A note on the text

The first listed publications of *The Adventures of Tom Sawyer* are the American Publishing Company's edition, Hartford, 1876, and the Chatto and Windus edition, London, 1876. A great many editions have appeared since then, the text used by the author in this edition being taken from the Signet Classic reprint of the Harper and Row hardback. This text has a short but thoughtful afterword by George P. Elliott and the events in each chapter are given in useful summary form in the list of contents. Details of this text together with those of other recent paperback editions worthy of recommendation are given below:

The Adventures of Tom Sawyer, Signet Classic, New York, 1959.

The Adventures of Tom Sawyer (Puffin Book), Penguin Books, Harmondsworth, 1950.

The Adventures of Tom Sawyer, New Windmill Series, Heinemann, London, 1961.

The Adventures of Tom Sawyer (Queen's Classics), Chatto and Windus, London, 1959.

Part 2

Summaries
of THE ADVENTURES OF
TOM SAWYER

A general summary

The Adventures of Tom Sawyer is the story of a few months in the life of
a young boy living in a small town in South-West America, on the banks
of the Mississippi River. The boy, Tom Sawyer, is both clever and
adventurous, often finding that the way in which adults go about
things is wrong and, on occasion, helping to correct their mistaken view
of the world. Tom lives with his Aunt Polly and his half-brother Sid;
the two boys have been adopted by their aunt on the death of their
mother. Aunt Polly is a very kind, elderly lady, determined to bring up
her two nephews to be good citizens. However, Tom, with his love of
adventure, finds himself using his wits to avoid many of the things
which Aunt Polly tries to force on him and she, in turn, often finds herself forced to admire the spirit of her 'naughty' nephew.

Tom befriends the son of the village outcast, a child of about his own
age named Huckleberry Finn. Huck is able to live the sort of life which
Tom admires very much, a life free from visits to church, baths, stiff
collars and all the other uncomfortable aspects of civilised life. The
two boys meet in the local graveyard one night, intending to bury a cat
in an attempt to cure warts. Normally, Tom has to indulge in 'make-
believe' adventures to enliven his existence. But, in that dark graveyard,
he and Huck witness the murder of the local doctor and find themselves
in the midst of a real adventure. They are the only ones who know the
true identity of the murderer and, when an innocent man is arrested,
the two frightened boys, with a third friend, Joe, leave the village and
hide on Jackson's Island. The villagers believe that the boys have been
drowned and are very surprised when the three reappear just in time to
hear the preacher delivering a funeral oration for the 'dead'. The boys
immediately become local heroes and, when the innocent Muff Potter
is about to be sentenced for a murder he did not commit, Tom stands
up in court and reveals the true identity of the murderer, an Indian
called Injun Joe. Injun Joe is in court, but escapes.

Tom is very frightened in case Injun Joe comes after him and tries to
kill him but, as time passes, his fear lessens. Later in the summer, he
goes on a picnic with his sweetheart, Becky Thatcher. The two get lost
in a maze of caves and again the villagers begin to think that Tom must
be dead. In the caves, Tom sees Injun Joe, who is visiting the site of his

buried treasure. Tom eventually finds a way out of the caves and returns with Becky to the village. There he hears that the main entrance to the caves has been closed off, and he realises to his horror that Injun Joe must be trapped inside. The villagers hurry to the caves and find the body of the murderer, who has been trying to hack his way out of the death-trap.

Some days later, Tom again returns to the caves, this time with Huck, and together they dig up the buried treasure. When the village discovers that Huck is rich, it immediately makes plans to civilise him. He is adopted by the Widow Douglas and the novel ends with Tom trying to persuade Huck to suffer the indignities imposed on him by this well-meaning lady, just as Tom puts up with the things that Aunt Polly forces on him.

Detailed summaries

Chapter 1

The book opens with Aunt Polly looking for Tom. She finds him, only to lose him again before she has had time to punish him for stealing some jam. He tricks her into looking the other way and, having made good his escape, does not reappear until supper-time. Although he has cleverly concealed the fact that he has been swimming, his younger half-brother, Sid, notices the one small flaw in his dress and exposes Tom's guilt. To avoid further trouble, Tom leaves the house, only to encounter immediately a boy who is the direct opposite of all the things he is himself. This boy, well-dressed and well-behaved, makes Tom feel shabby and annoyed, so he challenges him to a fight, beats him, then chases him home. He then returns to Aunt Polly's house and is discovered trying to creep indoors. The chapter ends with Aunt Polly determined that Tom will suffer for his sins the following day, a Saturday holiday.

COMMENTARY: This chapter serves to establish the normal pattern of Tom's daily life. It shows the reader the sorts of relationships he has with his aunt, his half-brother and his 'enemies'. Aunt Polly emerges as a simple, well-meaning woman who loves her nephew dearly, in spite of his naughtiness. Indeed, she actually admires the inventiveness that he shows in tricking her, even though this admiration conflicts with her desire to make him conform to the socially accepted modes of behaviour. Sid is seen as a rather self-satisfied and unadventurous character, quite the opposite to his half-brother, whose faults he is always trying to expose. Tom himself strikes the reader as a likeable villain, a boy who is undoubtedly clever but who uses his wits to avoid doing what is expected of him rather than putting them to more conventional use. He is 'wicked' in an engaging and harmless way.

At the very beginning of the book Twain establishes that the dialogue, which is fast-moving and colloquial, is as important as the passages which are written in the narrative voice. That voice tends to go to the other extreme; it is very literary and polished, a complete contrast to the dialogue, dialogue which is a very successful re-creation of the manner in which the people in the South-West speak. The way in which the words are spelt reflects the way in which they are pronounced, for instance 'ain't' for 'are not'. The narrator adopts a language which is refined and not at all colloquial, thus establishing a deliberate distance between the characters and the narrator. This and other effects of using such a narrative voice are discussed at length under the heading of 'Language and style' in Part 3. For the moment, it is sufficient to notice that there is this contrast and that it is used both to achieve a comic effect and to emphasise the vigour and vitality of the native, or colloquial, speech in the passages of dialogue.

Just as Twain uses two different levels of language, the narrative and the colloquial, so, throughout the book, he uses two different levels of meaning. The book is both about the youth of Tom Sawyer and about the youth of America, the nation. This duality is much more obvious in the sequel to this novel, *The Adventures of Huckleberry Finn*, but it is also of relevance in a discussion of this work. Tom Sawyer is young, and his youth, innocence and energy reflect the qualities possessed by America itself in this pre-Civil War period. As a nation, America is also young, energetic and innocent, still striving to find an identity, still able to question and even reshape the conventions on which the older world of Europe depends. For a further discussion of this parallel between Tom and America, see Part 3. For the moment, the student would be well advised to remember that, while the story is about the adventures of a boy, its significance does not end there and that what Tom says and does is often a reflection on the nature of the society in which he lives as well as an expression of his own buoyant personality.

NOTES AND GLOSSARY:
All the words glossed are colloquial unless they are followed by (*American English*), which indicates that they are standard expressions used in American English.

state pair: (*American English*) the pair (of spectacles) reserved for important occasions

stove lids: (*American English*) large iron discs fitted into the top of a wood-burning stove

I lay: I promise, I swear

the beat of that boy: anyone to surpass that boy

"jimpson" weeds: (*American English*) also called 'thornapples'; thorny, poisonous bushes growing to a height of five metres

the slack of his roundabout: the loose material of his jacket

truck: (*American English*) rubbish, mess

I'd skin: I would strip the skin from (as hunters treat the corpses of their prey)

hang the boy: damn the boy

ain't: has not

'pears: appears

get my dander up: (*American English*) annoy me

a lick: (*American English*) a blow, physical punishment

spile: spoil

Old Scratch: the Devil

laws-a-me: Lord help me

I let him off: (*American English*) I forgive him

most breaks: almost breaks

hooky: truant; playing hooky: absenting oneself from school without permission

obleeged: obliged

barely in season: (*American English*) scarcely in time

kindlings: (*American English*) small slivers of wood used to light (or kindle) a fire

revealments: revelations

middling warm: moderately warm

warn't: was not

powerful warm: very warm

knew where the wind lay: knew how things stood, understood the position

pumped our heads: pumped water over our heads from the pump

a singed cat: (*proverb*) implying one should not judge from appearances

better'n: better than

I wish to geeminy: (also 'jiminy') I wish to goodness, I wish very much

I'll lam: (*American English*) I will hit, I will strike

I'll learn him: (*American English*) I will teach him

citified: (*American English*) sophisticated, showing the influence of the city

smart: (*American English*) clever

you can lump ... if you don't like it: (*American English*) take it or leave it

dasn't: dare not

sass: (*American English*) impertinence

don't you crowd me: (*American English*) do not push me too far, do not annoy me

turned tail: (*American English*) retreated

Holler 'nuff!:   shout 'Enough!', admit defeat
in high feather: very pleased with himself, proudly
to 'lay':   to wait in ambush

Chapter 2

Saturday dawns bright and promising for everyone except Tom, who, to pay for his sins of the previous day, is being made to paint a fence. He soon puts his mind to the matter and, by making fence-painting seem a desirable way of spending a Saturday morning, manages to trick some of his fellows not only into painting the fence for him but also into paying for the privilege.

COMMENTARY: Again, the emphasis in the chapter is on Tom's clever-ness, the way in which he uses his wits to avoid doing those things which he finds boring or unpleasant. Here, he clearly emerges as far cleverer than his fellows, the 'innocents' who come to laugh at him but who end up working for him. The sorts of goods with which they pay for the honour of painting the fence are, of course, a comic catalogue of things to which no one save a small boy would attach any value. But notice how the children succeed in finding excitement and value in things which adults cast aside. This not only reveals how different their sense of values is to that of the adults; it also shows them as highly imaginative in finding uses for the useless.

Tom's success in creating a demand for fence-painting may also be taken as a wry comment on the capitalist system. Tom is an instinctive entrepreneur, or commercial intermediary, and a very good one, not only making a positive profit but also gaining, in the sense that he is relieved of a boring task without losing the credit for doing it.

The chapter also gives the reader his first sample of Negro dialect. Jim tends to shorten all his words, for example, master becomes Mars, old's final letter becomes a silent 'e' in ole, fooling and round also lose their final letters, becoming foolin' and roun'.

The character of Jim is seen to be as simple and as innocent as that of the village children, although Jim is, of course, not a child. His sim-plicity reflects his lack of formal education and, whilst it is obviously wrong that he, and his race, should have been deprived in this way, Jim does gain the benefits of extended childhood, benefits which Twain shows throughout the book. Jim plays a larger role in *Huckleberry Finn* and it is obvious, in this novel, that Huck (and the reader) are forced to recognise his basic humanity and to respect his many fine qualities.

NOTES AND GLOSSARY:
Mars: master
ole: old

tole:	told
git:	get
dis:	this
wid:	with
'spec:	expects
gwine:	is going to
ax:	ask
'tend:	attend
gimme:	give me
an tar de head off'n me:	(*lit.*) and tear the head from me; a forceful threat of punishment
'deed:	indeed
whacks:	hits
a white alley:	a prized species of marble (a game played with small, round balls or marbles)
a bully taw:	a winning marble
dat's:	that is
personating:	impersonating, pretending to be
stump:	capstan, place to tie up a boat
bight:	loop of a rope
druther:	would rather
honest injun:	(*lit.*) honest Indian, truly
how I'm fixed:	(*American English*) my predicament
awful particular:	very fussy, has high standards
lemme:	let me
fagged out:	exhausted

Chapter 3

Tom announces the successful completion of his fence-painting task to Aunt Polly. Until she sees it for herself, she is doubtful about his claim but, seeing it, is very pleased by what she takes to be proof that her nephew is not wholly bad. As she is in the middle of praising Tom, he steals a doughnut and leaves, throwing a few stones at Sid in passing. Having played a game with his friends, he starts for home again, only to plunge suddenly headlong into love when he catches sight of a new arrival in town. He starts to show off before his new love and is rewarded with a flower. He returns home in high spirits but is immediately in trouble, first for having thrown stones at Sid and then being unjustly beaten for breaking a sugar-bowl actually broken by his half-brother. He is so upset by the injustice of all this that he starts to imagine a world without Tom Sawyer, a world in mourning for the loss of one whom it had not loved enough. Lying outside the window of his new-found love, Tom's despair is only increased when a maid opens the window and tosses the contents of a pail of water over him. He returns home in the depths of despair.

COMMENTARY: This chapter shows the reader another side of Tom's character. When all is going well, then he is at ease in the world. When things go wrong, he takes refuge in a world of fantasy, a world familiar to any of us who, as children, have felt unappreciated or unloved. Tom is seen to be the possessor of a powerful imagination, the force behind all his clever tricks, which is now being used to a different end, to try to make Tom himself feel a little happier.

Up to this point, Tom's moments of despair have been short-lived and soon dispelled by the appearance of some new attraction. Here, however, he touches the heights and the depths. He falls in love and is rewarded with a flower. Before the day is done, he has fallen from this giddy height of love and hope into despair and thoughts of death.

Twain is carefully and cleverly controlling the reader's sense of perspective here. Whilst we can, in one way, sympathise with the boy's feelings in this chapter, on the whole, the vision of Tom, wet and prostrate beneath the window of his lady-love, is comic rather than tragic. His notion of the whole world mourning his death is, objectively, out of all proportion to what has actually befallen him but, to a small child, a minor set-back *can* assume the proportions of major tragedy and there is no reason why such a child's feelings should not be taken seriously. This question of perspective is a major one in the novel and is dealt with under the heading of 'Perspective' in Part 3.

NOTES AND GLOSSARY:

powerful seldom:	very rarely
hooked:	stole
I'll tan you:	I will slap you hard
showing off:	(*American English*) posturing
clodding:	throwing handfuls of earth (clods)
catch it:	(*American English*) be punished

Chapter 4

It is Sunday and Tom is trying to learn some passages from the Bible, his scripture, by heart. His efforts are unsuccessful, until he is offered a reward by his cousin. His performance immediately improves. Having been made to wash properly and been dressed in clothes which he detests, Tom goes to church and makes the best of a bad job by entering into another business deal. This time he collects tickets, proof of successful scriptural performance at Sunday school, in exchange for various treasures. None of the boys appreciate the value of their tickets until Tom, in sight of his new lady-love and her parents, steps forward with sufficient tickets to earn him a Bible and great praise. His cleverness, however, leads not to fame but to public humiliation for, when he is asked a simple question about the Bible, a subject on which, according to the number of tickets he possesses, he is an expert, his actual ignorance is revealed.

COMMENTARY: In this chapter Twain is doing two things. Firstly, he is showing that Tom's cleverness is not quite perfect. When he goes too far, then he is liable to be discovered. Secondly, in this and the succeeding chapter, he is taking the opportunity to be humorous about the religious observances of the small American town, talking of Aunt Polly as if she were an Old Testament prophet and noting how the superintendent has a special voice for Sundays. This point is discussed in greater detail in the commentary on Chapter Five.

It is significant that Tom, who is critical of all the things he is asked to do, should fail to see the point of learning passages from the Bible by heart. Only when he is offered some more immediate reward does he see any reason for undertaking the task. This attitude, the desire for immediate rather than delayed reward, is not so much mercenary as practical. As a rule Tom hates wasting time. He also hates the washing and the clothing that accompany visits to the church. His discomfort in the special Sunday clothes reflects his more general discomfort in any situation where he feels his natural self is being repressed; the clothes are parallel, in the restrictions which they impose upon his movements, to the more abstract restrictions imposed by Aunt Polly and the other adults who wish Tom to follow the conventional patterns of behaviour, patterns which to Tom, and often to the reader too, seem to have little basis in common sense.

NOTES AND GLOSSARY:

sure enough:	genuine
thickheaded:	stupid
'put him to rights':	tidied him up
yaller:	yellow
lickrish:	liquorice; a sweet, edible plant
spread himself:	showed off, sought public approval

Chapter 5

In this chapter we see the townspeople of St Petersburg at prayer. Twain describes them all in a gently mocking way and shows that they are in church not to listen to the sermon but to see and be seen by each other. The sermon is boring, even to the adults, and they are glad when a dog enters the scene and provides some diversion by engaging in a battle with a beetle.

COMMENTARY: The chapter serves to fill in more of the background detail of Tom's world. It shows a place populated with people who all know each other, a small world. Twain makes great play with the minister, emphasising how false and affected he is, standing in the pulpit using an odd voice, praying for things and places far beyond the knowledge of the people in the church and preaching a sermon which interests Tom for quite the wrong reason, namely, that it has a child as the figure leading men to salvation. Those repressed by European monarchies and Oriental despotisms, who are mentioned in the prayer, are very remote indeed from the congregation in St Petersburg and Twain exploits to the full the comic incongruity between what is said and where it is said. He also underlines how the people listening to such high-sounding but irrelevant words are really feeling somewhat repressed themselves, forced to assume unnatural attitudes of solemnity and piety, attitudes which soon begin to give way when the dog enters and goes through some amusing antics which leave the people desperately trying not to laugh and spoil the solemn effect of the occasion.

NOTES AND GLOSSARY:

thrown up to them: held up to them as an admirable example
as if she were cut glass: as if she were very fragile
sociables: (*American English*) social events
notices: (*American English*) announcements
pinch bug: an insect with pincers

Chapter 6

The chapter opens on Monday morning with Tom trying to discover some good reason to evade school. He convinces himself that he is ill, starts to groan and alarms both his aunt and Sid, who thinks that he is dying. Unfortunately, when he claims to be suffering from a decaying toe, Aunt Polly realises that he is not ill, for this is a very unlikely complaint. Tom then makes matters worse by mentioning a genuine but slight toothache; almost immediately he finds his aunt extracting the tooth. All, however, turns out well, for the loss of a tooth gains him the admiration of his school fellows. Before he reaches school, Tom meets Huck Finn, the son of the local drunkard. Huck is the envy of all the village boys, for his life is free from all the restrictions under which they suffer. No one cares sufficiently about Huck to make him go to school, or wash, or go to church. The boys become involved in a conversation about the best way to cure warts, concluding that the best way is to bury a dead cat beside some recently deceased evil-doer. They arrange to meet at midnight and try the cure and satisfactorily conclude their meeting by exchanging Tom's tooth and a tick. Tom arrives late at school and is challenged by the master. Tom notices that there is an empty seat beside his beloved, so he admits that he was talking to Huck, well aware that this awful confession will result in his being forced to sit amongst the girls, something which is intended as a humiliation. Sitting next to Becky, Tom is free to make overtures to her, impressing her with his ability as an artist, arranging to teach her to draw at lunchtime and telling her that he loves her. This meeting between the lovers is interrupted by the teacher, who separates them. Tom, however, is so happy with the progress he has made with Becky that he is unable to concentrate on his lessons and loses his place as the cleverest boy in the class.

COMMENTARY: In this chapter we see, in concentrated form, the pattern of Tom's life. It is a series of losses and gains; he loses a tooth only to gain renown and a tick, he loses his position in the class only to gain the favour of Becky, and so on. This pattern, one step forward and then one step back, is a small-scale reflection of the pattern of adult life. Tom has the advantage over any adult, however, that he recovers very quickly from reverses, completely forgetting them whenever he takes a step forward.

In this chapter Tom's running battle with the forces of convention is continued. He speaks to the local outcast and admits that he has done so, for he sees Huck not as a bad influence but as an admirable and wise figure. What to the adult eye looks like a poor, deprived and even delinquent child seems to Tom the epitome of romance, free from the system which entraps both children and adults. It is only when the boys return from Jackson's Island in a later chapter that Tom realises, when he sees that no one has missed Huck, what value there is in love, concern and care. They are more than just attempts to smother the spirit; they reflect the value of the person who is cared for.

In his courtship of Becky, Tom shows himself as clever as he is at all other things. He catches her attention by pretending to hide what he is doing and then, when her defences are lowered, he makes his confession of love.

NOTES AND GLOSSARY:

joggle:	(*American English*) shake about
rubbage:	rubbish
mortified:	(*American English*) decayed
hogshead:	(*American English*) a type of large barrel
spunk-water:	stagnant water
becuz:	because
she witched pap:	she put a spell on my father
stiddy:	steady
tick:	(*American English*) a small, blood-sucking insect

Chapter 7

The chapter opens with Tom suffering every moment of the morning in school, longing for midday and his meeting with Becky. To pass the time, he takes out the tick he has just acquired from Huck and starts to play a game with his neighbour Joe and the insect. Again, Tom becomes so involved in the game that he fails to see the master approaching. Lunchtime does eventually come, and Tom sets out to establish some common interests with Becky before introducing her to the idea of getting engaged to him. He is successful and their compact is sealed with a kiss. When Becky asks exactly what it means to be engaged, Tom is foolish enough to let slip the fact that he has been engaged before. Becky is distraught and will not be comforted, even when Tom offers her his greatest treasure.

COMMENTARY: Again we see the pattern of advance and reverse, of success and failure. The courtship between Tom and Becky is comically quick, perhaps reflecting rather humorously on the long, tortuous process which adults usually go through before making such agreements. In a sense, Twain is parodying romantic entanglements and their attendant emotions. But this does not mean that the feelings of the children are to be totally dismissed, for they are very acute. So the children both amuse us and engage our sympathy in their suffering.

The fact that the morning in school is spread out over two chapters indicates, of course, that Twain wishes us to feel, with Tom, just how slowly time passes. The time-scale between Chapters Five and Six was much longer, in fact, but was compressed, for the time passed quickly for Tom, being the night between the weekend and the dreaded Monday. Thus Twain carefully arranges his material so that the reader comes to feel as closely as possible as the central character feels. This point is discussed in the section on 'Perspective' in Part 3.

NOTES AND GLOSSARY:
ain't shucks to: is nothing compared to
slathers: lots, a great deal
blame it: damn it (mild curse)

Chapter 8

Tom is very depressed by his failure with Becky, so he sets off for the woods which have been attracting his attention all that morning through the school window. As he goes, he wishes that he might die, both to get some peace and to make everyone realise what they have lost. He cannot bring himself, however, to wish for a permanent death, for he is too fond of life and so has to compromise by wanting a temporary death. His spirits are restored for a time when he decides that he will become a pirate, then they are dashed again when he finds that a deeply-held belief about buried marbles multiplying is false. He meets Joe and soon forgets all his worries in a game of Robin Hood, a game in which the boys show that they have a fairly sound grasp of the story of this heroic outlaw and a reasonable notion of how he spoke.

COMMENTARY: Tom's flight from an unfriendly civilisation, where he is both a failed scholar and a failed lover, is, in a sense, symbolic of a return to less demanding, more natural, surroundings. Once there, he uses his imagination to transcend unpleasant reality, becoming a pirate and then Robin Hood. This childish ability to escape from reality via the imagination is lost to an adult who has allowed himself to be convinced that reality lies only in everyday situations which must, at all costs, be faced. Twain is here reminding us, through Tom, of what we have lost in losing our innocence. The 'elastic heart of youth' is a very sound and resilient organ indeed.

Tom's vision of his own 'temporary death' is, of course, amusing and an acute piece of observation on Twain's part. Most people recall having, as children, imagined punishing the ungrateful world through their own death. Thus Twain has accurately recalled one of the many facets of childhood. But Tom is not overestimating his importance to the world in his imaginings. On the two occasions in the book when he does suffer 'temporary death', that is, when he disappears and is assumed dead, then the world of St Petersburg does suffer just as much as he could have wished.

The significance of the game of Robin Hood is clear. Robin Hood was a legendary British outlaw and popular hero, a man who was supposed to have been cast aside by an evil king and who then spent his time robbing the rich to give to the poor. Thus, although he was opposed to the existing social order, Robin Hood had right on his side. It is clear why Tom, who is forever at odds with society, should choose to identify with this outlaw. Living in the woods, being free from society and yet doing some good are all things which appeal to Tom.

NOTES AND GLOSSARY:
a jog: (*American English*) a run
blamed mean: very mean

Chapter 9

From living in a world of make-believe adventure, Tom moves into real-life adventure. He and Huck meet as arranged and go to the cemetery after midnight. The pair are very frightened by the wind and the shadows, but when they see some actual men approaching, they are absolutely terrified. They are trapped and have to watch as Muff Potter and Injun Joe rob the grave in order to give the local doctor a body on which to experiment. The doctor refuses to pay the men any more than they have asked. Potter is knocked unconscious and Injun Joe kills and robs the doctor. When Potter recovers, his partner tells him that he, Potter, is the murderer. Potter's wits are usually affected by drinking too much, so he is ready to believe what Injun Joe says. Potter runs away, leaving Injun Joe triumphant.

COMMENTARY: Twain dramatically and effectively plunges Tom from fantasy into fact. The hero of the woods becomes a very frightened child and even Huck, who is accustomed to roaming about the world alone, is badly shaken. The practice of 'body-snatching', that is, removing the recently dead from graves for the purposes of medical experiment, had been common in Europe since the fourteenth century and was obviously transported to America along with many of the other malpractices of the Old World.

NOTES AND GLOSSARY:

scat:	go away
sperrit:	spirit
these-yer:	these here
done:	do not know
goners:	dead men
budge:	(*American English*) move
kin:	can
cussed:	accursed
pard:	partner
blubbering:	crying
chicken heart:	(*American English*) coward

Chapter 10

The terrified boys run back to town as fast as they can, where Tom realises that they are the only people, apart from the murderer, who know the truth of the matter. Huck knows, from experience with his father, that the drunken Muff Potter is not likely to be dead, so they are burdened with this awful knowledge. They agree that neither of them must say anything about the matter and Tom, with his book-inspired knowledge of such serious affairs, decides that they must swear secrecy in writing and sign the document with their own blood. No sooner is this serious business completed than their peace of mind is again disturbed by the appearance of a stray dog, an animal which, according to their superstitions, indicates that someone is going to die. They are greatly alarmed, fearing that their end is near, until they realise that Muff Potter is lying asleep nearby and is the attention. Tom returns home and goes to bed, unawar in the same room, is only pretending to be asleep. Tom morning to find that no one has bothered to waken hin has gone. When he goes downstairs, he longs to be punishe night absence, as revealed by Sid. For once, Aunt Polly ond giving him a 'licking' and her evident sorrow only adds to his already great burden of guilt. On reaching school, he finds waiting for him the treasure which Becky has spurned, and this is the final blow. He gives in completely to despair.

COMMENTARY: It is interesting that Tom should have recourse to fiction even in the face of fact. The idea of signing the oath in blood is taken from one of the many tales of adventure that he has read and it seems that, by imposing this fictional act between himself and the reality, he derives some comfort. More extensive discussion of Tom's relationship to literature appears in Part 3 under the heading of 'Tom and literature'.

The pattern of events which has existed so far in the book, namely, a fairly even balance between advance and reverse, is broken at this point. Tom's world collapses around him until every aspect of his existence is in disarray. He is so dispirited that he does not even want to take revenge on Sid for revealing his night-time exploits.

NOTES AND GLOSSARY:

faze:	kill
drownding:	drowning
to squeak 'bout:	to talk about
blab:	confess
to keep mum:	(*American English*) to remain silent
orter:	ought to
verdigrease:	verdigris
swaller:	swallow
just old pie:	blameless
dad fetch it:	damn it
bleeve:	believe

Chapter 11

The town is in a state of great agitation when the body of the doctor is discovered. Everyone crowds into the cemetery, including Injun Joe and Muff Potter, and Joe places the blame for the deed firmly on the shoulders of the latter. Tom feels a great sense of personal guilt, aware that he could have cleared Potter's name. A week of disturbed sleep is attributed, by Aunt Polly, to reaction to the murder. Tom's sensitivity heightened to the extent that he cannot bear the games being played by the village children, games modelled on the impending trial of Potter and centred on the deaths of cats. Tom derives some small comfort from going regularly to the jail to visit Potter and give him gifts.

COMMENTARY: The dramatic irony of the situation in this chapter is very pronounced. Aunt Polly's explanation of Tom's restless nights is, of course, very near to the truth, although she does not realise just how intimately her nephew was involved in the actual murder. The dead cats on which the children perform inquests serve only to redouble Tom's suffering, for it was a dead cat that brought him to the cemetery that fateful night. Again, the world seems to be conspiring against Tom, everything reminding him of what he is trying so hard to forget. For once, even literary models fail to offer him any relief. He is trapped by grim reality.

Chapter 12

Tom's worries about the murder are replaced by worries about his beloved Becky; she has stopped coming to school. These worries have, however, much the same effect as his previous ones and his apparent ill health makes him the victim of Aunt Polly's well-intentioned, but unpleasant, folk-remedies. His spiritual sufferings have physical suffering added to them in the shape of cold baths, diets, and so on. Under all this pressure, Tom becomes indifferent, but this merely makes his aunt redouble her efforts. At last, Tom is shaken from his lethargy and is forced to use his wits to avoid the distressing medical regimen. He doses the cat with the medicine being forced on him by his aunt and, when the animal reacts violently, he uses the opportunity to show Aunt Polly just what torment she is subjecting her nephew to. She is faced with the question, 'If it is cruel to subject the cat to this, is it not also cruel to subject Tom to similar treatment?'. He is somewhat cheered up by the success of this plan and returns to school to find that Becky is there. Unfortunately, all his attempts to attract her attention come to nothing, so he is once more depressed.

COMMENTARY: Twain uses Tom's illness as a way of poking fun at the sorts of amateurish remedies so prevalent in the country districts of the time. He also shows us a child teaching an adult something about the nature of caring, a reversal of the normal roles and proof, once more, of Tom's fundamental cleverness. However, Tom is not fully restored to his normal state for, whilst he enjoys his trick and its success, only this one area of his life shows any improvement.

NOTES AND GLOSSARY:

rot: (*American English*) nonsense

whistle her down the wind: put her out of his mind
thout: without
going on: (*American English*) behaving like
drift: (*American English*) meaning, intention

Chapter 13

Tom, feeling very depressed and unwanted, meets Joe, who is in a similar frame of mind after being unjustly accused of stealing cream. The two decide to abandon all attempts at living within the confines of society and, having enlisted Huck, they arrange to leave town to take up careers as pirates. Late at night, equipped with some stolen food, they get on board a small raft and make for Jackson's Island, an island in the river below town. At first they are quite happy, making fires and eating, discussing the ways of pirates and planning to be pirates who do not steal. But when they lie down to sleep, each of them feels a little worried. Tom and Joe feel guilty about stealing the food and neither of them is sufficiently 'wicked' to omit saying his prayers, even though there is no one present to force this ritual upon them.

COMMENTARY: Tom and Joe over-dramatise the extent to which they are unwanted and once more Twain is juggling with the perspective of the reader, who sees the over-dramatisation, and of the boys, who take themselves seriously. The situation must indeed be serious for Tom, because once more he translates what he has read in books into action; the last time he did this was when he signed the solemn pact. The gaps in his knowledge of pirates make the whole enterprise rather comical, as does his insistence that things should be done in the least convenient, but most unlikely, ways. But beneath the surface comedy there is a more serious point. The boys, with their vigour and spirit, have finally been driven from the social rut and are, in a sense, returning to the wilderness, seeking their true, as opposed to their social, identities. The situation is new, even to Huck, who is accustomed to living on the fringes of society.

NOTES AND GLOSSARY:
take up: (*American English*) restart
bullyrag: tease, torment
bulliest: best, greatest
fitten: fittingly
sniffing around: exploring, investigating

Chapter 14

Tom wakens to find himself close to nature, surrounded by insects and birds. The three boys pass a happy morning, doing just what they choose. In the middle of the afternoon, their peace is disturbed by a series of booming noises which turn out to be coming from a cannon mounted on the ferryboat. The whole village is out searching the river for the bodies of the three boys, dropping bread containing mercury into the water then letting off a cannon in the hope that, as folk-wisdom maintains, the bodies will rise to the surface. Tom and his friends are delighted with the whole performance, especially as they are the object of the hunt, but, when night begins to fall and the boats depart, they begin to feel lonely again and to think of those on shore who will be missing them. Joe tries gently to suggest that it might be time to go home, but he is dissuaded. When Huck and Joe fall asleep, Tom creeps away from the camp, leaving his treasures and a note behind him.

COMMENTARY: The chapter opens with a long passage in the narrative voice, a passage describing Tom against the background of nature and showing the two to be in complete harmony. The Tom whose little world has been subject to pressure from those larger than himself, namely the adults, now has his world to himself and, in an unconscious parody of the adults, he begins to take an interest in the world of things smaller than himself, the insects. But unlike the adult humans, Tom does not try to alter or destroy the little world of these creatures; he merely observes closely and admires. When the others awaken, the idyll is continued. They catch fish and swim and are utterly contented with their aimless existence. Again, Twain is making the point that children are much closer to nature than adults, who, in a similar situation, would no doubt be trying to escape from the island and arranging their time usefully.

The appearance of the boats from the village serves, at first, merely to divert the boys and to add to their sense of adventure. They watch the spectacle, entranced. However, when night falls and the spectacle vanishes, the boys are left to confront the fact that they have left people behind, people who are worrying about them. Once more, civilisation and the ties of love and duty intrude and sour the sweet taste of freedom. Tom, with his usual fundamental approach to things, decides to return to the village to see just what the situation there is, instead of spending a night tormenting himself with imaginings.

NOTES AND GLOSSARY:
feeler: tentative suggestion

Chapter 15

Tom swims ashore and hides aboard a ferryboat going to St Petersburg. He darts through the village and enters his Aunt Polly's house unobserved. She is sitting with Mrs Harper (Joe's mother), Sid and Mary, the women dwelling lovingly on the boys they have lost and Sid trying to put the departed Tom into a less flattering light. Tom discovers that the village believes them to have been drowned because the empty raft on which they went to the island has been found. He also discovers that, whether or not the bodies have been found, a funeral service will be held for the boys on Sunday. After Mrs Harper has left, in great distress, Tom is confronted by the spectacle of his aunt praying for, and crying over, her lost nephew. He waits till at last she has fallen asleep, goes to her bedside intent on leaving a comforting message when, suddenly, another idea strikes him and he merely kisses her gently on the lips, then sets off back to the island. He arrives just in time for breakfast, and in time to prevent Huck and Joe dividing up his treasures between them.

COMMENTARY: The initiative which Tom shows in getting back to St Petersburg is still further proof of his cleverness and his enterprising approach to life. From his hiding place in his aunt's house, he witnesses some very touching scenes of grief, being forced to face the suffering which he has caused. But he does not immediately put a stop to that suffering by appearing, possibly knowing that to appear at such a moment might well result in punishment rather than a welcome. Or, possibly, he feels that the adults have not learned their lesson thoroughly enough as yet; they might still be tempted to interfere in the old way if their suffering is short-lived. Thus Tom is strong enough not to let the pity that he feels for his aunt override more practical considerations, a kind of behaviour which would do credit even to an adult.

NOTES AND GLOSSARY:
breathed himself :   recovered his breath
harum-scarum: (*American English*) erratic, unpredictable
cretur: creature
true-blue: (*American English*) honourable

Chapter 16

The days continue to pass, but by Friday Joe's spirits are so low that neither swimming nor treasure-hunting holds any appeal for him. He just wants to go home. Both Tom and Huck are feeling a little depressed, too, but Tom refuses to let either of them give in and, just as Huck and Joe are wading into the water on their way home, he lets them into a 'secret' which persuades them to stay, a 'secret' which he has been saving for just such an emergency. They return in much better spirits and after supper Tom and Joe decide to try smoking like the 'sophisticated' Huck. Both are very sick as a result of this and eventually they fall asleep, only to be awakened by a terrific thunderstorm, which terrifies and soaks them and leaves them feeling very depressed and homesick once again. A game of Indians succeeds in making the following day pass quite well and in the evening they settle down once more to pursue the newly acquired art of smoking.

COMMENTARY: In this chapter Tom's power as a manipulator of men emerges very clearly. He has saved the 'secret', just as he hid his presence in Aunt Polly's house, until the right psychological moment. The storm appears to continue the pattern of advance and reverse, a pattern which has continued to bedevil Tom even on the island. Twain uses it to show the reader the boys in a new light, drawing back from the three heroes so that we are once more aware that they are merely three little boys alone in the wilderness.

NOTES AND GLOSSARY:
dumps: (*American English*) depression
hendering: hindering
tobacker: tobacco

Chapter 17

While the boys are enjoying the game of Indians, the village is in mourning. Becky is wandering about wishing she had been kinder to Tom and all the other children are trying to get some glory by claiming acquaintance with the dead heroes. On the Sunday, the visit to church is even more sombre than usual. Mr Sprague devotes all his powers of rhetoric not to the European monarchies but to the great qualities possessed by the three boys. As things reach a climax, with everyone in tears, the boys (who have been hiding in the gallery, listening to their own funeral sermon) appear in the church and are greeted with even more tears. Tom notices that Huck is the only one who is not being smothered in kisses and the kindly Aunt Polly immediately turns her attention to him, making poor Huck even more embarrassed than before. The people sing a hymn of praise and the whole village forgives the boys for the suffering which they have caused.

COMMENTARY: The chapter shows that Tom was very accurate in calculating the effect which their reappearance in the middle of the funeral oration would have. The 'secret' which he used to keep Huck and Joe on the island was just this, that they were to be 'buried' on Sunday. Tom also proves his basic humanity by forcing people to take note of Huck as well as of himself and Joe. It would seem, from the reactions of the adults, that they have successfully learned the 'lesson' which Tom was trying to teach them.

NOTES AND GLOSSARY:
sold: (*American English*) tricked, fooled

Chapter 18

When things have calmed down a little, Aunt Polly gently upbraids Tom for having caused so much suffering and for failing to think of those at home. Tom tells her of the night he returned to the house, but he pretends that he dreamt the events rather than actually witnessing them. His aunt is so overjoyed on hearing that Tom 'dreamt' that he kissed her that Tom begins to feel very guilty about this new 'trick'. However, he sets off for school and enjoys walking through the town, the centre of attention wherever he goes. At school, he pretends to ignore Becky and concentrates instead on his former love, Amy. Becky tries to recapture his attention by going round issuing invitations to a picnic, but when even that fails, she makes Tom jealous by paying attention to Alfred, the 'citified' creature with whom Tom fought in an earlier chapter. Unfortunately, all that happens is that Tom and Becky find themselves forced to endure the attentions of Amy and Alfred respectively. Becky casts Alfred aside when the disappointed Tom leaves and Alfred, in a fit of rage, spoils Tom's spelling book. Becky sets off to tell Tom but then changes her mind.

COMMENTARY: In this chapter we see, once again, the pattern of advance and reverse, of gain and loss. Tom has gained the admiration of the whole town, but he has still lost Becky, so his happiness is spoiled. Twain is continuing, through the figures of Becky and Tom, to make fun of the tortured courtships of adults, courtships which are usually full of such mutual misunderstandings.

In telling the lie to Aunt Polly, about having dreamt of the scene between Mrs Harper and herself, Tom is running the same risk as he ran with the 'ticket trick'. What he does is open to discovery by the adult world and it is a piece of miscalculation on his part. Having got away with so much, he cannot stop himself from overdoing it and so he is leaving himself open to more trouble.

NOTES AND GLOSSARY:

the beat of that: anything to better that
giddy: (*American English*) thoughtless, impetuous
make up: (*American English*) become friends again, forget a quarrel
pretty thin: (*American English*) rather dubious, suspect

Chapter 19

Tom is confronted by his aunt, who is furious. She had been so eager to let Mrs Harper know that Tom was a good child, and one who had marvellously accurate dreams, that she had gone there immediately after being told the lie. Mrs Harper, of course, had been told by Joe that Tom had been home, so all was revealed. Tom feels bitterly ashamed and even when he does tell the truth, that he came to comfort his aunt, he has lost all credibility. She is touched, however, by the idea that he might have wanted to kiss her and almost believes him. When he has gone back to school, she confirms his story by finding the undelivered piece of bark on which he wrote his message.

COMMENTARY: Tom learns a valuable lesson from all this. He knew, just as soon as he lied, that he had done something wrong in playing on the credulity of his simple, but kindly, old aunt. However, he has to face the suffering he has inflicted in the shape of a sorely disappointed Aunt Polly and he is forced to recognise that adults, too, have their feelings and these must be respected whenever possible.

NOTES AND GLOSSARY:
an old softy: simpleton
kept mum: (*American English*) remained silent

Chapter 20

Tom returns to school feeling much better now that his aunt knows the truth but his spirit is soon dashed when he meets an unfriendly Becky. She accidentally tears the schoolmaster's private book on anatomy when Tom is present. The two children sit down, both wondering what will happen. Tom works it out that Becky will be found guilty, for her guilt will show on her face. After he has willingly accepted the punishment for his ink-stained book, Tom sees the master take out the book on anatomy. As the man questions each member of the class, Tom is desperately wondering how to save Becky. When it is her turn to be questioned, he leaps up and claims that he was responsible and takes yet another beating from the master, as well as two hours' additional school work. His reward is Becky's admiration and her confession that Alfred was responsible for the ink-stain on Tom's own book.

COMMENTARY: Tom begins the chapter in happy mood, suffers a reverse, but in the end is happy again, having won Becky's love. His actions in saving her from the punishment which she dreads are evidence of his good nature, for he cannot be certain that she will not rebuff him even after he has made this gesture. The reader is aware of all the undercurrents in the situation but the master, the representative of the adult world, is ignorant of all but the most superficial aspects. Twain exploits this 'dramatic irony' to remind the adult reader that too hasty a judgement of what is going on in the world of children is often wrong. The children's world is all but closed to the adults in the novel, but the reader is in the position of seeing things from the other side, from the child's point of view, and so has a much broader perspective.

Chapter 21

As the holidays approach, so too do the examinations, so the children are forced to live under an even harsher regime than usual at school. Naturally, they plan to take revenge. When the Examination Evening comes, the time when the children are publicly examined by the master in front of the whole town, the children have a plot worked out, a plot which takes account of the fact that the master is usually slightly drunk on such occasions. As the master tries to draw a map on the blackboard, a cat is lowered from the attic above onto his head. The frightened creature seizes the master's wig and reveals, for all the town to see, his bald and gold-painted head, the paintwork having been done whilst he slept.

COMMENTARY: In this chapter, Twain continues to show what monsters adults are, or can be. The master is quite merciless and unjust in his punishments. But, as is usual in this novel, when an adult steps out of line, the children succeed in teaching him a lesson, thus neatly reversing the normal order of things.

Twain also uses this chapter to mock yet another American ritual, the prize-giving speech. He has already made great fun of the sort of rhetoric used by the preacher and the superintendent in the church. Here he makes fun of the meaningless and worn-out phrases which the children are made to learn. Their speeches do not reflect what they think but what they are supposed, in a very idealistic way, to think. And the sentiments are expressed in the most false and artificial way possible. Twain uses actual examples of speeches in his attack on this tradition of forcing children to say things which they do not mean or even understand, and the fact that the examples are drawn from real life lends added conviction to his attack. Education is seen as stifling and warping the natural spirits of the children, as punishing them without reason and as teaching them arts which are not worth acquiring.

Chapter 22

Tom tries to enliven his holidays by joining a local organisation which allows him to wear a bright uniform if he gives up drinking and swearing, but he finds this too tedious and abandons it before he has even had the occasion to appear in public in his finery. Other attractions come to town, but their appeal also fades. Then Tom is taken ill, and emerges after a fortnight to find that everyone, including Huck, has been 'converted' into a moral and religious being. He returns to bed that night, only to be scared by a thunderstorm which he fears is an attempt by God to kill him, the only unreformed character in the town. As a result of this fright, he suffers a relapse and spends another three weeks in bed. When he emerges once again, things are back to normal; the passion for religion has passed.

COMMENTARY: It becomes obvious almost at once that the school, whilst it is usually regarded as a prison by the children, is a very necessary feature of their lives. It provides them with excitement when they escape from it and fills in a great deal of time, time which otherwise hangs heavy on their hands. Twain extends the reader's impressions of the background in this chapter, showing the small and remote community being visited by a number of diversions, such as a circus, but being, for the most part, a rather dull place in which to live.

During the thunderstorm, Tom is referred to as an 'insect' on a piece of turf when he lies amid the thunder, believing that God has sent it down on him alone. The remark itself reminds us of Tom's earlier interest in the world of insects on Jackson's Island, an interest which at that point seemed to parallel the interest of the adult in the world of the child.

Chapter 23

The dull summer is enlivened by the start of the murder trial, but for Tom this is also a trial. He takes Huck aside to ensure that he is still resolved not to say anything, but the two boys find themselves dwelling on all the kind and harmless things which poor Muff Potter has done. They visit Muff Potter, only to be made to feel even more guilty because he regards them as his only friends. On the last day of the trial, when Potter's fate seems to be sealed, Tom confesses the truth in court and Injun Joe confirms his own guilt by making an escape.

COMMENTARY: This scene is a real test of Tom's character. If he can stand by and allow the adult world to see justice miscarried, he will be no better than that world. But, as he has shown throughout the book, he is highly critical of the way that world works, so it is not surprising that in the end he does stand up and put the adult's view of things to rights. His essential goodness is proved beyond a shadow of a doubt, for he risks his own life by his action; he knows full well that he is risking death at the hands of Injun Joe.

NOTES AND GLOSSARY:

som'ers:	somewhere
hain't:	has not
warn't:	was not

ketch:	catch
lynch:	(*American English*) hang without trial
furder:	further

Chapter 24

After the trial, Tom is greeted as a hero by all the village. He enjoys this, and the gratitude of Muff Potter, who is also being treated as a hero. But the nights are dreadful. Tom lives in constant fear of Injun Joe, and Huck Finn, although Tom did not name him in court, is disillusioned at the breaking of so solemn an oath.

COMMENTARY: Yet again, the pattern of loss and gain is evident here. Tom has gained fame and a clear conscience, but he has lost peace of mind and the friendship of Huck.

Chapter 25

Tom decides that it is time to go hunting for treasure. He enlists Huck's aid by assuring him that robbers often bury their spoils, only to die before they can recover them or forget where they have left them. The three likeliest locations for treasure are haunted houses, islands and beneath dead trees. They set off, armed with shovel and pick, to the nearest dead tree. Resting beneath it, they discuss what they will do with the money when they find it. Huck, whose ideas are limited to buying a soda every day, is appalled to hear that Tom plans to marry when he has the money, but he feels a little better when Tom assures him that Huck will live with the newly-weds.

After they have been digging for some time, Tom remembers that the treasure will be where the shadow of the dead branch falls at midnight. They return then, but have no greater success, so decide to turn their attention to the haunted house, but not at night, when the ghosts are likely to be about.

COMMENTARY: Tom's ideas about treasure-hunting are clearly derived from the books he has read, books which deal with the old, and much-dug, earth of the Old World rather than the virgin soil of the New. However, this does not enter his considerations and he sets about his task, convinced that he cannot fail. Huck, who respects Tom's learning, is given a few lessons in the course of this chapter. He finds out where treasure is likely to be hidden, why it is there, what diamonds are and what kings get up to. All this 'knowledge' is drawn from fiction; but in return Huck offers Tom a piece of advice, based on hard experience. He knows that women are bad; they always fight with men and destroy them, for this is what his mother did to his father.

The reader should recognise that Huck's lack of formal education does not make him inexperienced. Indeed in the book bearing his name, Huck's common sense contrasts well with Tom's imaginative and largely irrelevant way of going about things.

NOTES AND GLOSSARY:

mighty particular: very specific
ha'nted: haunted, occupied by spirits
a raft of 'em: a great many of them
thish-yer: this here
sure-'nough: real
more lonesomer: lonelier
shadder: shadow
to a dot: precisely, exactly

Chapter 26

The boys meet again the next day, but have to put off their visit to the haunted house because it is Friday, a very bad time to go near a haunted house. They meet again on the Saturday and enter the house, frightened but determined. Whilst they are upstairs, two men come into the house, one of them the 'mute' Spaniard, who turns out to be Injun Joe in disguise. The boys stare with horror at the men through a hole in the floor. Trapped upstairs, they can only watch as the other two settle down to wait for the night to fall. Just before the two men leave, they decide to hide their money and, in doing so, come across a box containing thousands of dollars. The boys are overwhelmed with delight, but it is short-lived, for the two villains decide to take the money away and bury it in den 'Number Two'. They are suspicious, for they have found Tom's pick with fresh earth on it, but a search of the upper floor is abandoned when the stairs collapse. When they go, the boys emerge in a state of terror, for Injun Joe has spoken of 'revenge' and they suspect he means revenge on them. They go home.

COMMENTARY: Twain in this chapter exploits the nature of boys' adventure stories. The most unlikely things can happen in such stories and the events in this chapter are certainly unlikely. It is, of course, for readers who have become involved in the story, a very tense moment, with Huck and Tom in the threatening presence of Injun Joe, hidden in a haunted house, trapped upstairs and in a dreadful position.

NOTES AND GLOSSARY:

been a brick: (*American English*) been a great or admirable character
yew bow: a bow made from the wood of the yew tree

budge:	(*American English*) move
shanty:	broken-down place
to stir out of here:	to move out of here
leg it:	walk it
swag:	booty, goods got by stealing
den:	hiding place

Chapter 27

Tom wakens the next morning, hoping that he dreamt the events of the previous day. However, when he meets Huck, he knows that they were real. The boys work out that den 'Number Two' must be a room in a local inn, so they decide to keep watch on it and follow Injun Joe if he emerges.

COMMENTARY: Twain tries to compensate for the unlikely nature of the events in the last chapter by making Tom himself doubtful of their reality and unable to grasp the idea of so large a sum of money. Tom once again shows his courage by insisting that they should follow Injun Joe.

NOTES AND GLOSSARY:

dog'd:	(also 'doggoned') may I be cursed (if I do not do something or other)
lemme:	let me
track:	(*American English*) follow a trail
foller:	follow

Chapter 28

Huck watches the tavern for four nights until it is dark enough for Tom to enter the room. He does so and emerges from the place at a great speed, telling Huck to run. When they reach safety, he says that Injun Joe is in the room, lying in a drunken sleep on the floor. The room itself is full of bottles, a secret store of drink in a place which officially does not serve alcoholic drinks. The boys do not have the courage to return and search the room, so they part, Huck going off to sleep in a barn, with strict instructions to keep watching the room every day and night.

COMMENTARY: Twain builds up the tension in this chapter by forcing the reader to stay with Huck when Tom vanishes into the room. He also extends the picture which we have of Huck, the homeless boy who has to sleep in barns but who is liked by the Negroes because he treats them as human beings. Huck also shows unswerving loyalty to Tom, being determined to continue his watch on the place in spite of his fear.

The fact that Injun Joe is taking refuge in a Temperance Tavern, in a room filled with drink, is another attack by Twain on the gap between the official and the actual morality of the adult world.

NOTES AND GLOSSARY:
scary: frightening

Chapter 29

Tom is cheered by the news that Becky has returned from her holiday and the long-awaited picnic is to take place the following day some distance down the river. It is agreed that Becky should spend the night at the Harpers' house, but Tom suggests that they go instead to the Widow Douglas's home after the picnic, for she has ice-cream. Tom remembers that Huck is still on the trail of Injun Joe but decides to forget him for the moment. After the picnic, the children take candles and set off to explore the caves. Time passes quickly and the children are late returning from the caves to catch the ferryboat. They arrive back tired at the landing-stage. Meanwhile, Huck is on guard and sees the two villains emerge from the room carrying what he takes to be the box of treasure. He decides that there is no time to call Tom, so he follows them himself. They go to the house of the Widow Douglas, where it is clear from what they say that she is the victim of their intended revenge. Injun Joe means to attack and disfigure the woman who has been good to Huck, just because her husband has been responsible for humiliating Joe publicly. Huck creeps away, then runs for help to the nearest house. It is owned by the Welshman and his sons. On hearing Huck's story, the men set off towards the widow's home, while Huck runs off in the other direction.

COMMENTARY: Huck Finn emerges from this chapter with considerable credit. Like Tom, he seems to have a natural moral instinct, one which will not allow him to see an injustice done to the widow. The picnic scene allows Twain to give the background of the caves. Injun Joe's chief grievance against the late Judge Douglas is that the Judge sentenced him to be punished in the same way as Negroes are punished, by public whipping. It is this, more than anything else, which has aroused Injun Joe's resentment, for even he regards himself as being better than the slaves. The reader, Huck and Tom know that this is not the case, and again the standards of the adult world are seen to be faulty, allowing even the worst of white men to assume their superiority over the black.

NOTES AND GLOSSARY:
jugg'd: put in jail

Chapter 30

On Sunday, Huck returns to the house where he went for help the previous night. It belongs to a family of Welshmen. They greet him as a hero and welcome him in, but have to tell him that the men escaped from them in the dark. Huck has great difficulty in explaining why he is following the men and why he was out at that time of the night in the first place. His story breaks down under questioning and he admits that the 'Spaniard' is Injun Joe. He makes the old Welshman promise not to say that he had anything to do with it, then he is taken ill. The Widow Douglas, who does not know how much she owes to the boy, is called in to nurse him. Meanwhile, at church it is discovered that Tom and Becky did not return with the others from the picnic and a search of the caves is begun at once. After three days the children are still missing.

COMMENTARY: Huck, who has been coming into even sharper focus over the last few chapters, finally falls ill from the years of neglect that he has suffered. But this illness does not occur until he has done a great deal of good. When questioned by the Welshman, Huck lacks Tom's ability to tell consistent lies, but this only makes him more admirable.

The adult world is in turmoil at this point. The Temperance Tavern has been closed, now that the drink has been made common knowledge; the whole village is under threat from an escaped murderer and most of the men are away searching for the children. The two children who usually keep the world on a steady course, Tom and Huck, are absent or ill. Things are happening very quickly, in complete contrast to the dull start of the summer, and Twain is making an admirable job of keeping several complicated threads of the plot under control.

NOTES AND GLOSSARY:

acrost:	across
a jiffy:	(*American English*) a split second, an instant
a posse:	(*American English*) a group of men gathered specifically to seek a criminal or criminals
blowed on them:	exposed them
shackly:	ramshackle, broken down
dogged:	followed closely
widder:	widow
flighty:	behaving erratically
beholden:	(*American English*) indebted

Chapter 31

We return to the day of the picnic, and follow Tom and Becky further and further into the caves. At last they realise that it is a long time since they heard other voices. They turn to go back but discover that they are lost. Becky breaks down, but is comforted by Tom and they renew their attempts to get out. They lose all track of time, sleeping and resting, eating the few crumbs of food that they have. At one point, they are exploring a side-corridor when Tom sees a human hand with a candle appearing. He is about to shout with joy, till he realises that it is the hand of Injun Joe. He goes back to Becky, who is weak by this time and convinced that she is going to die. He kisses her, but will not stay by her side. He goes off on another search.

COMMENTARY: The narrative in this chapter is superb, describing the fear of the children in a most effective way. Tom is, as usual, showing great courage, but things are so bad that even he is almost without hope by the end.

Chapter 32

The chapter opens with Mrs Thatcher and Aunt Polly ill with despair, believing Tom and Becky to be dead. Then the two are found and brought to the village, where everyone comes to shake their hands. It appears that Tom's final attempts at exploration had led him up a tunnel which ended on the banks of the river five miles away from the village. He and Becky had been rescued and restored to their relatives by two men who happened to be going down the river on a skiff. Tom and Becky are ill for a short time, and Huck is still in bed in a poor way. At the end of the chapter, Tom discovers that the entrance to the caves has been closed off, and he immediately tells Judge Thatcher that Injun Joe must be trapped inside.

COMMENTARY: Where the last chapter moved slowly, allowing the reader to feel the time weighing as heavily upon him as it did upon the children, this chapter is filled with incident. Tom emerges from it very well, for he persuaded Becky to go on living in the cave and then rescued her. His place in the village is assured.

Chapter 33

Injun Joe's body is found just inside the door of the cave. Tom feels pity for the man whose death was so like what his own could have been. However, he is also glad that the threat of the murderer has been removed, and Injun Joe enjoys a kind of immortality, for the entrance to the cave is always associated with him, marked by the hole in which he collected water. His funeral, too, is quite an event, so his end is more glorious than his life. Tom persuades Huck to get out of his bed and come back with him to the cave, for he has realised that the money must be hidden there. They find the money under a rock and, returning to town, are caught by the old Welshman, who takes them to a party in Huck's honour. The widow intends to adopt Huck and educate him, but he is saved from this fate by Tom, who brings in the money which they have found, half of which belongs to Huck.

COMMENTARY: The narrator is more in evidence in this chapter. He wonders aloud about the drops of water which kept Injun Joe alive for a few days, drops which have fallen there for millions of years. He asks, 'Has everything a purpose and a mission?' and then dismisses the question and turns his attention to a group of ladies who had been pressing for Injun Joe's release. These he describes as 'weaklings'. (The role of the narrator in this and other chapters is extensively discussed in Part 3, under 'Language and style'.) Here, Twain seems to be preparing his readers for the end of the story, taking over from the characters as the chief means of communication.

The characters themselves, however, still have a lot to do. The boys are frightened in the cave, but comforted by the sight of a cross inscribed on the rock covering the treasure, thus showing that they do not only have their own 'alternative' religion of superstitions (also discussed in Part 3) but that they subscribe to the adult religion when it is useful to them.

Tom is already returning to 'normal'. Having been through such awful adventures in the caves, he still plans to use them as the site of future imaginary exploits, like piracy. This shows his resilience and his ability to transform things through the imagination.

When they return to the village, poor Huck is forced to clean himself up and wear a suit of clothes bought for him by the widow. This, like Tom's Sunday clothes, is a form of restriction on his natural freedom of movement.

NOTES AND GLOSSARY:
nipped: stole
it's a whiz: it is very exciting

Chapter 34

Huck is appalled by the way in which the village seems to be taking him over. He tries to persuade Tom to escape from the waiting crowd, but Tom says they must go down to the party. When they get there and Huck's part in saving the widow is narrated, she decides that she will educate him and adopt him. Tom is aware of what a threat this well-intentioned woman is posing to Huck's freedom so he steps in to save his friend by revealing the extent of Huck's wealth.

COMMENTARY: This chapter shows that Tom is very much aware of how

Huck feels. He knows what it is like trying to live under the adult system, and he admires Huck for the freedom he possesses. So he uses his wits to resue his friend from what, to the adults, seems like a good fate but what, to Tom and Huck, seems like a kind of imprisonment.

NOTES AND GLOSSARY:

slope: (*American English*) escape
blowout: (*American English*) feast
scrape: (*American English*) difficulty, danger

Chapter 35

The narrator sums up the whole story, saying that Tom and Huck are village heroes, that every haunted house is searched for treasure by the adults, showing how every word spoken by the boys is listened to and their past histories rewritten to conform with their present status. Judge Thatcher plans a great future for Tom, the Widow Douglas invests Huck's money for him and Huck, in spite of Tom's efforts, is dragged into society. He bears this for three weeks, then returns to the barrel in which he used to live, away from the monotonous regularity of life with the widow, the cleanliness and barrenness of 'civilised' existence. However, Tom persuades him to give life with the widow another try by saying that, to be a member of his gang, Huck must have a certain social standing. Huck decides that he will manage to endure civilised life if he has the release of being a robber in Tom's gang. The book ends with the boys planning another terrifying ceremony with oaths, blood and all the rest, and with the narrator saying that he must stop at this point before the boys become men.

COMMENTARY: This last chapter makes even more explicit the criticism which Twain has of the adults' way of ordering the world. Huck, who has become a person we admire, finds their way of life intolerable. But Tom, who is aware that the adult world will not let the wealthy Huck go, manages to arrange a compromise, introducing Huck to the world of the imagination, a realm where the boys may live as they please and where they may escape from the adults' regime.

NOTES AND GLOSSARY:

chaw: chew tobacco
to shove: to leave
bar'l: barrel
tollable: tolerably, quite
shet: shut
crowd through: succeed
bust: burst

Part 3

Commentary

IN HIS PREFACE to *Tom Sawyer*, Mark Twain said it was 'intended mainly for the entertainment of boys and girls', but added that he hoped it would not be 'shunned by adults on that account'. These remarks were made in response to the insistence of his wife and a fellow writer, W.D. Howells, that he should not openly maintain that the book was not for children. This conflict of views, and Twain's subsequent concession to the opinions of those he respected, are germane when we come to ask ourselves whether or not the book is 'merely' a children's story. Clearly, the author himself meant the work to appeal to adults rather than children and, this being so, the surface level of the book is not necessarily the level at which it was intended to produce an effect. On the surface, it is a story for children, a story full of adventure, of adults proved wrong, of children as heroes. On the surface, the book moves along at an easy and a humorous pace, passages of dialogue being interspersed with the comments of an ironic narrator. However, when we begin to seek beyond this surface level, to search for the profounder aspects of the work which will make it of interest to adults, then we are in great danger of being too cleverly analytic, of finding things which are not there. In the course of the discussion so far, the areas into which the novel strays at this deeper level have been indicated but at no point in the book itself are these deeper concerns made explicit. Certainly, there is a connection to be made between the youth of Tom and the youth of the American nation. The book is not, however, in any sense a parable for the fate of the American sensibility. Twain did write a novel of much deeper import on this topic in *Huckleberry Finn*. He did not choose to do it in *Tom Sawyer*.

Because this deeper level, the level which we might suppose necessary to engage the adult mind, is so little in evidence in *Tom Sawyer*, it might be best if we look at what we have got, the surface level, in greater detail. Accepting the novel as it stands, in all its simplicity, what interest does it hold for the adult? Firstly, it is a good 'yarn', a story which grips the imagination without making too many demands on the intellect, a story whose surface meaning is immediately clear and in which the pace of the narrative is sustained at a fairly fast rate. This immediate impact should not be discounted when we are seeking the appeal of the book to the adult mind, for sophisticated taste is not necessarily a distinguishing feature between man and boy. Secondly, the book presents the adult reader with a picture which is full of nostalgia. It allows him, through the insights we get into Tom's view of the world, to re-enter the world of childhood, a world for which we all, as adults, retain some kind of longing. Thus, we have the dual attractions of entertainment and emotional appeal to justify the book's claim to the attentions of the adult.

Thirdly, we have something which is very closely related to this return to the world of childhood: the book presents the adult reader with a view of the world seen through the clear and uncompromising eyes of the child. This childlike vision is, in a sense, primitive, unaware of the finer points, untroubled by responsibility, by such notions as planning for the future. But to call this vision primitive is not to condemn it. It is, rather, to recommend it. Twain not only reminds us of how we once were; he also, through the medium of Tom and Huck, shows us what we have lost and what we have become. Lost is the intensity of emotion, such as Tom feels for Becky. Lost, too, is the tremendous capacity to become so involved in another project that great sorrow is soon forgotten. Tom is, above all else, resilient, overcoming his problems and worries, not through the exercise of intellect, nor through the sort of institutionalised solace offered by the Church, but through his sheer zest for life. His wish for death is for a 'temporary' death.

So Twain shows us what we have lost in terms of intensity and resilience. He also shows us what poor shadows of our promising younger selves we have become. Although Aunt Polly is well-meaning enough, she is rendered almost helpless by the conflicting pulls of her love for Tom and her desire to bring him up within the conventional structure of society. As a result, she punishes him erratically, feeling obliged to do so because she wants him to grow up with a certain view of the world, a view hedged about by moral rules, and notions of social acceptability and usefulness. At the same time, she is reluctant to curb his spirit and even admires his enterprise and his daring. Through Aunt Polly, Twain shows his adult readers how shaky, how confused and how illogical are the grounds on which they base their actions and their decisions. The religious notions which govern Aunt Polly are worth no more (and perhaps less) than the superstitions which govern the lives of the children in the book. The superstitions have at least the advantage that the outcome will be visible in this world, in the immediate actuality, rather than in some future world whose shape is extremely uncertain. Heaven and hell are ideas which persecute both adults and children, but adults have not the child's capacity to work their way around the notions and so to arrive at some comfortable and convenient compromise.

This is where the fascination of the book lies for the adult reader, in this picture of the world from an angle which reveals the folly, the illogicality and the sheer discomfort of the 'grown-up' way of ordering existence. It is significant that none of the adults enjoy life in the way in which children do. These children suffer at times and, proportionately, their grief is as great as any adult grief. Yet they recover quickly and continue to derive a great deal of pleasure from their world. Only when convention, in the shape of religious observance and social codes, enters the scene does life begin to be lived with less zest or joy. And, instead of showing us that the adult world, with its worries and responsibilities, is a more admirable place than the world of the child, Twain shows us the exact opposite. The adult world, with its money, its religion and its conventions, is no more moral, no more sensible and no more enjoyable than the world of the child, with its barter, its superstition and its fluid structure. Tom in the end proves his fundamental morality by risking his life to save Muff Potter and his fundamental chivalry by trying to protect Becky from the knowledge of her impending death. Neither of these things can be attributed to his training. They are inherent in Tom, the 'noble savage', who resists the pressures to conform, who does not listen to the canting of the preacher and who acts as he wants to act despite all threats.

In spite of the apparent 'depth' of this insight into the adult world, the novel is not a serious work. Twain was working within the humorous tradition, the tradition outlined at the outset of this book, and he remained true to it. If the adult world emerges from the novel looking a little foolish, then this only adds to the fun of the thing. It does not cast the shadow of serious intention across it. The book is heavily autobiographical, being based on Twain's recollections of his boyhood, recollections tempered by the forty years since his birth and by his fondness for the humorous vein. To reality, Twain added a dimension of fantasy. As in all good 'boys' stories', the book is full of unlikely adventures and coincidences, of gruesome sights and easily recognised bad or evil characters; it is also a book in which actions have no serious repercussions, save in the case of Injun Joe and the doctor. Tom survives the threat of Injun Joe, the rigours of the cave and a serious illness apparently unscathed and quite unshaken. His life, like summertime St Petersburg, is charmed, continuing unaltered in spite of evil, death and disappointment.

Thus the book might be classed as humorous fantasy, a hymn, as Twain himself put it, 'to simplicity'. Its purpose is not difficult to define. Humorous fantasy need do nothing more than divert and entertain, both of which this book does to great effect. If it also provokes a wry smile on the part of its adult readers, a smile which acknowledges that they, as adults, are part of a world for which the author and the hero have little respect, then this smile is no more than a tribute to the comprehensiveness of Twain's vision. He has, in this novel, very thoroughly recreated the feelings of a world of childhood, in all its bright, primary colours and its unquestioning acceptance of life. We who live in a world made grey by too great an awareness of our own mortality are made, for a moment, to laugh at our own seriousness, our standards, our rituals and our respectability.

The novel is set in the 1840s, about a decade before the outbreak of the Civil War which brought about the final destruction of Tom's world and the world of the South-West as Twain had known it in his childhood. Because it is a humorous fantasy and because its hero is a child, the social issue which was to prove so crucial to this world, the question of slavery, does not appear in the book. Tom treats the Negro, Jim, much as he treats his fellows and Huck at one point 'confesses' to eating with a friendly Negro. Apart from these two brief appearances, the Negro population does not figure in the book and there is no sign in it of Twain's great sympathy with that race. What does concern Twain here is the faintly ludicrous spectacle presented by people clinging to the edge of the wilderness and upholding all the standards of 'civilisation'. In both the scene in the church (Chapter 5) and the Examination Evening scene (Chapter 21), we are aware that Twain is making fun of what passes for religious observance and academic achievement amongst these simple and earnest people. As always in this book, his treatment of these matters is broadly comic; it is only when we come to *Huckleberry Finn* that we see him making a more serious comment about the dangers inherent in empty rhetoric which is unrelated to reality.

The basic plan

The basic plan of the novel is very simple. It follows the chronological progression of the events in Tom's life. On occasion, the time-scale is compressed so that the time passes quickly for the reader and for Tom; on other occasions, when Tom is going through a particularly painful experience (as in the caves), time is drawn out. Towards the end of the novel, when things are happening thick and fast, Twain temporarily abandons the straightforward time-scheme. In Chapters 29 and 30, Tom is left in the caves whilst the reader follows Huck through his adventures at the widow's house; then, in Chapter 31, we are returned to the caves a couple of days prior to the time at the end of Chapter 30. Chapter 32 opens after Tom has escaped from the caves and the intervening period is covered by his recounting of this escape.

Within this relatively uncomplicated time-scheme, Twain gives his readers a series of episodes, dwelling on the more important ones at some length, hastening over those which contribute rather less to the action of the story. His intention is clearly to sustain the interest of the reader by keeping things going at a fairly fast rate. This simplicity of plot and of structure reflects Twain's desire to model the book on other adventure stories for boys, stories equally simple in their basic design. By the lavish use of coincidence, Twain puts his characters just where they are needed at any given moment. It is a coincidence that Huck and Tom should be in the graveyard the night of the murder, it is a coincidence that the boys should be in the haunted house when Injun Joe appears there and it is a coincidence that Huck should be shadowing Injun Joe when the latter attempts to attack the Widow Douglas. Again, within the framework of a humorous fantasy, such coincidences are quite acceptable, for realism has no place in fantasy.

We now come to some of the aspects touched on in the commentaries on the various chapters. These aspects, together with the nature of the major characters (see below), are the most interesting features of the book and are worthy of close attention and study.

Language and style

From the very outset of the book, it is apparent that there are two distinct types of language being used, the colloquial language of the characters and the polished language of the narrator.

It was Twain's usual custom to allow the hero of his novels to take on the role of the narrator. He uses this device to great effect in both of his novels, *The Innocents Abroad* and *Huckleberry Finn*. In *Tom Sawyer*, however, he departs from this custom and allows the character of Mark Twain to do his narrating. There is a certain loss of immediacy in using this method, for the words are not those issuing from the child-hero and so we are not constantly exposed to his point of view. Twain compensates for this by recreating the feelings of his hero in a form which is only slightly more polished than the form which the boy himself would use. When he wishes to put forward his own point of view, then Twain makes the language more literary and polished and uses the distance between his language and the actual events being described to create a level of irony. All these aspects of the narrative voice are apparent in the following extract from Chapter 2:

> By the time Ben was fagged out, Tom had traded the next chance to Billy Fisher for a kite, in good repair; and when *he* played out, Johnny Miller bought in for a dead rat and a string to swing it with—and so on, and so on, hour after hour . . .
>
> He had had a nice, good, idle time all the while—plenty of company —and the fence had three coats of whitewash on it! If he hadn't run out of whitewash, he would have bankrupted every boy in the village.
>
> Tom said to himself that it was not such a hollow world, after all. He had discovered a great law of human action, without knowing it— namely, that in order to make a man or a boy covet a thing, it is only

necessary to make the thing difficult to attain. If he had been a great and wise philosopher, like the writer of this book, he would now have comprehended that Work consists of whatever a body is *obliged* to do, and that Play consists of whatever a body is not obliged to do. And this would help him to understand why constructing artificial flowers or performing on a treadmill is work, while rolling tenpins or climbing Mont Blanc is only amusement. There are wealthy gentlemen in England who drive four-horse passenger coaches twenty or thirty miles on a daily line, in the summer, because the privilege costs them considerable money; but if they were offered wages for the service, that would turn it into work and then they would resign.

The boy mused a while over the substantial change which had taken place in his worldly circumstances, and then wended toward headquarters to report.

In the first part of this extract, Twain uses language rather closer to the language of Tom Sawyer than the language he uses at the end of the extract. Such phrases as 'fagged out', 'played out' and 'bought in' are colloquial, the sorts of phrases which Tom himself would have used. So, in this early part, Twain is merely narrating Tom's thoughts and in doing so remains close to Tom's sort of language. When, however, we come to the reflections of the narrator himself, 'He had discovered a great law of human action,' then the language becomes less colloquial. In this paragraph, Twain is intent on using Tom's fence-painting exploits as a lesson for his readers, pointing out to them that there is a very fine distinction between what is considered to be work and what is called play. He is not, of course, entirely serious in making these remarks; they are witty and their wit is not directed at Tom so much as at the adult reader who lives in a world of such arbitrary distinctions. The point, however, is not a profound one, so when Twain calls himself 'a great and wise philosopher', he is extending the humour to include himself. He is ironical at the expense of reader and narrator alike. Only in the last, very short paragraph is he ironical at Tom's expense. By referring to Tom's 'worldly circumstances', Twain is making a little joke. The phrase suggests at least some wealth; what Tom in fact has, as the reader knows, is a collection of rubbish which includes a dead rat and a dog-less collar. So there is a gap between the 'importance' of the phrase and the actuality, a gap which is intended to be ironical, slightly mocking Tom's estimation of his own 'worldly circumstances'. When Twain refers to Aunt Polly's house as 'headquarters', he is again being gently ironic. No one could be less military than poor Aunt Polly, so the idea of her as the commander of troops, which is implicit in the word 'headquarters', is ludicrous and amusing. No doubt she herself

believes that she has attained some almost military stature by succeeding in making Tom work, just as Tom believes himself to be rich on
the basis of his rubbish. In both instances, Twain neatly suggests the
characters' views of their own stature, and how foolish it is, by using a
single word or phrase.

This is one of the major ways in which Twain creates a level of irony
in the book. He will use a word which, to the reader, seems far too
dignified, or literary, or grand for the actuality to which it refers. Yet
the word indicates the characters' own assessments of the actuality,
assessments which are often comically out of proportion.

At other times, Twain uses a much broader form of narrative humour.
In the passage quoted above, he makes very obvious fun of the 'English
gentlemen'; in Chapter 5, he treats the Reverend Sprague's method of
delivering the sermon in a similarly comic way and then goes on to
mock the practice of reading announcements from the pulpit: 'The
Rev. Mr. Sprague turned himself into a bulletin board, and read off
"notices" of meetings and societies and things till it seemed that the
list would stretch out to the crack of doom—a queer custom which is
still kept up in America, even in cities, away here in this age of abundant
newspapers.' This broader humour tends to appear when Twain moves
away from his central characters to deal with the wider world of the
village and of America. It is a means of putting the activities of Tom and
his friends in the context of this wider world and of showing that, even
in that world, things are comical, lacking a rational basis. Twain con-
cludes his remarks on Sprague's announcements by saying, 'Often, the
less there is to justify a traditional custom, the harder it is to get rid of it.'
This is a general comment on human folly, a comment casually dropped
into the midst of the narrative, which then returns to making mock of
Sprague.

A similar, broadly humorous narrative approach can be seen in
Chapter 21, which deals with the speeches on Examination Evening:

> A prevalent feature in these compositions was a nursed and petted
> melancholy; another was a wasteful and opulent gush of 'fine lan-
> guage'; another was a tendency to lug in by the ears particularly
> prized words and phrases until they were worn entirely out; and a
> peculiarity that conspicuously marked and marred them was the
> inveterate and intolerable sermon that wagged its crippled tail at the
> end of each and every one of them. . . . The glaring insincerity of these
> sermons was not sufficient to compass the banishment of the fashion
> from the schools, and it is not sufficient today; it never will be suffi-
> cient while the world stands, perhaps. There is no school in all our
> land where the young ladies do not feel obliged to close their com-
> positions with a sermon . . .

A pattern very similar to the one in the Sprague passage is evident here. Twain begins with a mocking comment on the immediate events in the book and then moves from these events to a more general condemnation of American customs. Here, as in the previous passage, he is intent on condemning language which is used to no good effect. Mr Sprague did not need to make the announcements. Nor do the young ladies need to make speeches full of insincerity. It is custom which dictates that both things should take place, and custom itself is mocked by Twain. The compositions referred to here are hymns in praise of America, or God, or education, hymns which in no way reflect the real feelings of their composers. This attack ties in with what we see elsewhere of the effects of civilisation on the young; it cripples and confines the imagination and replaces natural vitality with stale custom and insincere utterances. It is these sorts of things that Tom and Huck both resist. Tom's frequent escapes into the world of the imagination are his way of countering the stultifying effects of education and civilisation.

In conclusion, Twain uses the narrative voice in a variety of ways. He may narrate the feelings or thoughts of his characters, using their sort of language to do so; he may be gently ironic at their expense by inflating the language of the narrative beyond what the actuality demands or he may extend the scope of the book through the narrative, so that he moves away from his characters and dwells more generally on human folly. But, whatever the narrative voice may be doing, it is always done gently: the criticisms are phrased so that they seem amusing rather than harsh; the characters' aspirations are treated tenderly and so are their thoughts. The narrative voice, of course, performs a fourth function: it sets the scene and in doing so often reaches almost poetic heights:

> The drowsing murmur of the five and twenty studying scholars soothed the soul like the spell that is in the murmur of bees. Away off in the flaming sunshine, Cardiff Hill lifted its soft green sides through a shimmering veil of heat, tinted with the purple of distance; a few birds floated on lazy wing high in the air . . . (Chapter 7)

In contrast with the narrative voice, the language of the characters is fairly crude, but lively and vital. The children especially, with their enthusiasm for life, speak with vigour. They live among the extremes of experience, complete happiness or deep despair, total confidence or abject terror, and their language reflects this full-blooded approach to existence. Although 'bulliest', 'cracky', 'It's nuts,' and so on, may not be standard English, such words are very effective in creating an impression of genuine, childish enthusiasm.

In writing the passages of dialogue, Twain successfully recreates the *sound* of the words, altering the spelling so that it reflects the pronunciation. 'Are not' becomes 'ain't', 'do not know' becomes 'dono'; many words are shortened or telescoped in some way. When Jim appears in Chapter 2, there is a subtle difference in the way he speaks. His language has an even more marked tendency to abbreviate and he replaces 'th' with 'd': 'My! Dat's a mighty gay marvel, *I* tell you! But Mars Tom I's powerful 'fraid ole missis . . .'. This phonetic re-creation of language succeeds in giving the reader a more intimate insight into the characters. We see, in their words, something of the texture of their characters, the terror and credulity of Jim, the energy, terror and credulity of Tom, Huck and Joe, the nastiness of Injun Joe, the affected nature of Mr Sprague and the touching incompetence of Aunt Polly. All the qualities possessed by the characters and evidenced by their language stand out more sharply when contrasted with the literary tone of the narration.

Perspective

The word 'perspective' means the view of the world of any given perceiver. How that world looks depends very much on the nature of the person looking at that world and we have already noted, in the sections dealing with specific chapters, that there is a difference between the way in which the children in the book see events and the way in which the narrator and the reader see the same events. Twain exploits these three possible ways of looking at things, or perspectives, using them for a variety of purposes. Broadly, he is interested in exploring the gap between adult perspective and the perspective of the children and in using this gap to comic effect. In the very first chapter the question of perspective is raised when Twain remarks that the depressed Tom cheers up 'Not because his troubles were one whit less heavy and bitter to him than a man's are to a man, but because a new and powerful interest bore them down and drove them out of his mind for the time —just as men's misfortunes are forgotten in the excitement of new enterprises.' This comment shows us that Twain is not out to devalue the sufferings which Tom and the others endure but that he wishes the reader to realise that children, unlike adults, soon recover from setbacks which to them are serious. A certain zest for life, a deep interest in new experience and a consequent resilience are the main features of Tom's character. Thus, what to Tom appears very depressing strikes the reader slightly differently. Under the guidance of the narrator, we are well aware that sufferings will be of short duration and so we take them less seriously than the actual sufferer. While sympathising fully with the deeply felt emotions of any given crisis, we are also aware of the comic potential of such emotions, a potential which derives from their impermanence. In this way, Twain guides our perception of things, involving us yet allowing us to be amused.

Perspective is carefully controlled throughout the book. If, when Tom is lying grieving beneath Becky Thatcher's window, he seems an object worthy of our pity, the narrator will step in to lighten the gloom with some humour. Tom's sorrowful thoughts are rudely interrupted: 'The window went up, a maidservant's discordant voice profaned the holy calm, and a deluge of water drenched the prone martyr's remains!' It is not merely the fact that Tom is soaked which makes such an incident funny. Here, as elsewhere, the narrative voice deliberately overstates the case, describing the boy as a 'prone martyr'. Undoubtedly, Tom does see himself as a martyr at this point, but he would not describe himself in such a high-flown and incongruous way, so the words make him appear comic rather than tragic. Tom's view and the narrator's view are neatly arranged so that the perspective which the reader is forced to take on the matter is humorous.

However, the world and the outlook of the children are not always a source of laughter. Although treated lightly and with some humour, that world and outlook are not without value. If we look first at the world of the children, then we see that it mirrors the world of the adults, but with certain significant differences. Where the adults value money, the children value such things as dead rats, extracted teeth and little insects. The commerce which takes place in the adult world is reflected in the 'swapping' which goes on in the world of the children; but the difference is that the adults are dealing not with goods but with symbols, in the shape of money. The children deal directly with the goods themselves. And these goods are the sorts of things which the adult despises. The children are more discerning. Nothing, for them, is without its value; dead rats are not just horrid vermin but things which can be swung round on strings. Obviously, the adult reader will find this amusing, but he may also be reminded of a time when he, too, saw value in tiny, cast-off objects and he may even see that his relationship to 'things' has changed for the worse. Adults are much more selective and much less enthusiastic about their possessions.

The world of the children also mirrors the world of the adults in terms of human relationships. Adult male pursues adult female, so Tom pursues Becky. Again, however, there is a subtle difference, for the latter pursuit will not end with the capture of a lasting nature. Tom may wish to be married but this wish is based on nothing more than the vaguest of notions of what marriage is. He is, after all, an orphan, his aunt is unmarried, Huck's family life is non-existent and even Joe does not seem to have a father. So Tom can have little idea of what marriage is really like or what purpose it serves. His courtship of Becky is far from smooth and is productive of much suffering, but again the reader can treat this suffering as being amusing rather than tragic, for Tom is far too young to need a wife. What is impressive about the relationship between Tom and Becky is that it is pure and is based on nothing more than platonic love, on the desire simply to be with the other person. It has none of the ulterior motives of adult love.

Thus the children take the conventional aspects of the adult world, such as courtship and money, and translate these conventions into something much more basic and much simpler. Certain conventions, however, have to be endured rather than taken over and enjoyed. Going to church and to school are things which Tom finds tedious. At school, he makes the best of things and is an able pupil. Church, however, involves getting washed and dressed in restrictive clothing, and sitting for an hour or so, listening to a sermon whose irrelevance is obvious to Tom. The clothes parallel the conventions, in that both hamper his freedom and make him uncomfortable; at the end of the book, we see Huck being put into a similarly uncomfortable and unnatural position as the Widow tries to civilise him. He, too, is imprisoned in clothes, forbidden the pleasures of smoking and forced to wash. These illogical deprivations and discomforts affect him even more deeply than they affect Tom, for Huck has long been accustomed to being his own master. It is interesting that the novel should end with Tom trying to reconcile Huck to this imprisonment by introducing him to his own method of escape, the exercise of the imagination, the substitution of imagined experience for real tedium. Tom would appear to be an acute little fellow, well aware that the adult world has the final say in many matters and that some compromise of this sort is necessary.

Tom's superior grasp of reality is also evident in the fact that he values Huck long before Huck becomes wealthy. It is Tom who talks to Huck, Tom who involves him in adventures, Tom who insists that someone should be glad to see Huck when they return from Jackson's Island and Tom who tries to protect Huck from the villagers by telling them that Huck does not need to be adopted because he is wealthy. So the world which Tom inhabits does not despise people just because they live beyond the realms of normal society. Indeed, it is fair to say that the world of the children constitutes an alternative society, one which is much more humane, more enlightened and more comfortable than the society created and perpetuated by the adults. The parallel between the world of the children and the world of the insects has already been mentioned. On Jackson's Island, Tom takes great interest in the little creatures that climb all over him, but he does not interfere with them nor try to reshape their lives. In this, he sets an example for the adults in the book. They do not look on the world of childhood as Tom looks on the world of the insects. They try to shape and control the children, putting them in restrictive clothes, making them deliver speeches which are wholly false but satisfy the adults' idea of childish sentiments, and so on. We, the readers, have a privileged

insight into the world of the children and so we see that it is no less complicated and no less moral than the world of the adults. It is, in fact,
preferable to that world.

If we now turn to the outlook of the children, then we see that it is far
from simple. Tom does not reject the Church without cause. Sprague,
as Twain shows, has nothing to offer in terms of real insight into things
and that is why Tom rejects him and the conventional sort of comfort
he offers. On more than one occasion, Tom has to act as the corrector
of the mistaken views of adults. He teaches Aunt Polly a lesson about
the cruelty of dosing children with medicines and he teaches her another
lesson about injustice by disappearing to Jackson's Island. Of course,
he, too, has lessons to learn; his trickery with the Sunday school tickets
is exposed and his lie about the dream causes him to feel very sorry
indeed for abusing Aunt Polly's simplicity.

The outlook of the children is shaped by a number of factors. Firstly,
they like living and go into things wholeheartedly. Secondly, their
imaginations are highly developed, so they respond in a very vivid way
to most stimuli. Not only do they play games with a will; they actually
go out and look for adventure. This search, in Twain's St Petersburg,
is rewarded by the treasure. The place is obviously rather dull for the
adults, with nothing but church and Examination Evenings to enliven
their days. It is the children who provide the main source of excitement
by getting lost. The children themselves find excitement in unlikely
things, like looking for treasure. Thirdly, the children believe that there
is a hidden structure to the world, a structure which is magical and
sometimes frightening. Instead of following the rather dull ways of the
adults, they believe in superstitions of all kinds, hoping that buried
marbles will multiply, and knowing that witches will interfere in human
affairs. This means that the results of any course of action can be seen
within a very short time; if you bury a marble then dig it up, you know
whether or not witches have interfered, for if they have, then there will
still be only one marble there. This compares favourably with the
beliefs of the adults, beliefs which involve behaving in a certain way in
this life in the hope that you will be rewarded in the next. For the children, such hope is of little relevance, for the time-span between act and
reward is too great. So they substitute superstitions for religious beliefs.

This does not, however, mean that the children are immoral in their
behaviour. Whilst Tom rejects convention, he shows a fundamental
moral sense by helping Muff Potter and saving Becky from despair in
the caves. He also suffers guilt when he hurts Aunt Polly's feelings. So
the world and outlook of the children are to some extent modelled on
the world of the adults, but with certain differences which make their
world a better place and allow them to express their own, innate
morality as well as their natural high spirits.

From the perspective of the children, the adult world is often seen as lacking in common sense. People do things which are not enjoyable; they make mistakes and miss out on a lot of enjoyment. Duty and responsibility weigh heavy on poor Aunt Polly, who is constantly torn between admiration for Tom and her desire to curb his spirit so that he will grow up to conform: 'Tom got more cuffs and kisses that day— according to Aunt Polly's varying moods—than he had earned before in a year; and he hardly knew which expressed the most gratefulness to God and affection for himself' (Chapter 17). The glimpses we get of this adult world are very partial indeed, for we are only aware of what the children make of it and, occasionally, what the narrator makes of it. The latter usually seems to coincide with the children's assessment.

The perspective of the narrator has already been discussed under the heading, 'Language and style'. When Twain is not narrating the children's feelings, he often takes the reader beyond the immediate situation of the characters and puts the story against a wider background of human comedy, suggesting that the particular follies of St Petersburg are but examples of a general variety. At other moments, however, Twain makes subtle adjustments in the perspective of the reader, a perspective which he controls both through the characters and through the narration. For example, in Chapter 16, when the three boys are on Jackson's Island, he suddenly introduces a storm which makes the 'rural idyll' turn into a nightmare and forces us to see our three 'heroes' as lonely, frightened boys: 'The storm culminated in one matchless effort that seemed likely to tear the island to pieces, burn it up, drown it to the tree-tops, blow it away, and deafen every creature on it, all at one and the same moment. It was a wild night for homeless young heads to be out in.'

Thus we have the perspective of the children, where everything looms large and alive, the perspective of the narrator, which focuses on the comic side of things, and our own perspective, which is largely dictated by our exposure to the two other perspectives. We have a splendid insight into the world of the children and come to like and admire them. But we are also aware that they are a little comic, so we must compromise, as Twain meant us to, by adopting his stance of amused, but never condescending, sympathy. The book as a whole is a delightful, humorous, unlikely tale, which nevertheless has some bearing on reality. The outlook of the children is beautifully portrayed, from Tom's desire for a 'temporary' death to Huck's sour remark about marriage. The events may be unlikely, but the children are fairly realistically drawn and it is a pleasure to the reader to be reminded of the vivid joys and terrors of childhood; it is a lesson to him to be reminded of what he has lost in terms of innocence, and it is illuminating for him to see the adult world from the uncompromising perspective of that innocence and the equally uncompromising perspective of the narrator.

Tom and literature

In order to cope with some of the more galling restrictions imposed by the adult world, Tom takes refuge in a world of the imagination. And it is here that we see the link between the perspective of the narrator and the perspective of the child. That link lies in the exercise of the imagination. When needing to escape, Tom always uses routes already marked out for him in the books he has read. In the world of St Petersburg, there is little, save Nature itself, which warrants imitation. Instead, Tom imitates Robin Hood and pirates, seeks buried treasure and pretends to do all the things which he has read about. It is obvious that, no matter how much he may dislike it, school has given him something worthwhile, has opened up new avenues to him and offered him the chance to escape more effectively.

Of course, Tom himself, as a character, neatly fits several literary archetypes or models. When he falls so suddenly in love with Becky, then he joins the ranks of all lovers of literature; when he performs tricks for her, then he joins the ranks of the chivalrous gentlemen who, since medieval times, had ridden off to do great deeds for their lady-loves; when he is spurned by Becky, he merits a place with all the disappointed lovers in literature; when he takes charge of his 'band' on Jackson's Island, he joins all the great leaders of literature and myth; when he stands up in court to tell the truth, he is identified with all the heroic truth-tellers; when he succeeds in tricking adults or his fellows, then he earns a place amongst the admirable tricksters. More generally, as a young orphan, he may be placed alongside the fatherless children in the works of writers such as Charles Dickens (1812–70) and when he exhibits bravery, morality and natural affection, he may be seen as the 'noble savage', the untamed creature with an innate nobility.

However, Tom's place amongst these literary archetypes is not straightforward. It is perhaps part of Twain's ironic purpose that such myths should be glimpsed behind Tom; the figure in the foreground, being so young, looks slightly comic against such a backdrop. He is comical as a lover, precisely because he is too young to be a lover; he is comical as a leader of men, because his 'men' are Huck and Joe; and he is even faintly comical as a heroic teller of truth, for he does it signing the oath in blood. He is comical, too, as a trickster, for his tricks are on so small a scale. As an orphan, of course, he is not comical, but this status (which is ripe for exploitation in an attempt to make the reader weep over a parentless boy) is not exploited. Tom never mentions his parents and does not seem to miss them at all, so he is not tragic in his orphaned state.

So Tom both uses literary archetypes in order to make his world more exciting and, although he is unaware of it, fits into several literary archetypes himself. Finally, however, Tom Sawyer becomes a wholly new literary archetype, the young American boy who responds in so original a way to his world.

Tom and America

The connection between Tom Sawyer and America was mentioned in the Introduction. Tom is young and the America of his day had been a free nation for only seventy years, so it, too, might be accounted young. The freedom which America gained from the Old World was political and social. The nation, like Tom, had won for itself the freedom to make its own rules, within certain reasonable limits. However, as we see in figures such as Mr Sprague, Aunt Polly and Judge Thatcher, the people of America did not seem to want to take up this new opportunity. They remained within the well-worn grooves which they had inherited from the Old World. Mr Sprague's sermon and the speeches made on Examination Evening are the two specific comments which Twain makes on the way the American society is developing. Sprague's comments, in both prayer and sermon, are so remote from the kinds of everyday reality with which his congregation are having to cope. The prayer shows a certain pride in democracy, mentioning European oligarchies and other repressive systems of government in a slightly smug way. The references serve to remind the people of St Petersburg how lucky they are to be living in such a free society. Yet what they are doing with this freedom can be seen in the Examination Evening, when children make optimistic noises about democracy without ever questioning just what value it has, and in the attitude of Aunt Polly to Tom. She is constantly trying to curb his freedom in a way that is certainly undemocratic.

However, the similarity between Tom and America is not of major importance in this novel. The awareness that there is a parallel certainly adds to our enjoyment of the book, but Twain waited until writing *Huckleberry Finn* before making a much more explicit attack on what was becoming of the freedom offered to man in this new land. In this figure of Tom, we can see the possibilities for action outside the conventional social framework. The manner in which Twain portrays Tom makes us aware that actions such as his may well be preferable, more reasonable and closer to true human needs than the actions taken by those who are inhibited, as the adults in the book are, by notions of 'respectability' which are scarcely appropriate in their particular situation. Seen from this angle, it is possible to regard Tom as an 'ideal American'. He compromises with the needs of society but he is also flexible enough to respond to the less ordinary demands of existence on the fringes of the wilderness. So through him Twain is reminding us not just of what we have lost in taking the irrevocable step from childhood to adulthood; he is also pointing out to his fellow-countrymen what opportunities they themselves are losing in this New World by clinging to ideas derived from the Old World. As usual, however, the point is not made with any great seriousness. It is a slightly more profound, but still amusing, additional level of meaning.

The characters

Tom Sawyer

The character of Tom is evident in what he says and in what he does. His words, interests and actions all reflect his youth; he likes to play games, to live in a world made exciting through the exercise of his imagination, to avoid the things which he finds tedious, such as baths and trips to church. None of these things is particularly remarkable in a child, but the way in which Twain portrays Tom leads us to admire him. In playing games, Tom usually casts himself as the hero, but in real life too he is a hero, risking his own life to save Muff Potter and protecting Becky from despair in the caves. Thus Tom is in fact a very remarkable child; he is the possessor of an unusually quick intelligence, which he uses to make his own life bearable by injecting some excitement into it, and to teach the adults around him some necessary lessons about their own failings.

Tom lives in a world dominated by women. He is being brought up by his aunt, with the occasional assistance of his cousin Mary, and he loves Becky. Huck is threatened by female domination in the shape of the Widow Douglas, and Mrs Thatcher and Joe's mother figure much more in the book than either Judge Thatcher or Joe's father. Tom has, in a sense, to fight for his male identity, to prevent himself being smothered by the women around him, and he has also to play a male role, to take the initiative even with his aunt, who is older than he. Thus circumstances put Tom in a position where he has no man on whom he may model himself or to whom he must defer. He is free to find and to express his own nature. He responds to this challenge in a splendid fashion, for he has, as his aunt knows, a great deal of spirit.

Twain does not make Tom into too 'great' a character. Tom is a child, and so is afraid of all manner of things and is not altogether aware of the nature of adults. His fear appears especially during the two storms in the book, storms which suggest to him that his ultimate father, God, is displeased with him. His imperceptiveness about adults appears when he plays a trick on Aunt Polly and causes her real and unnecessary suffering.

However, given these humanising failings, the character of Tom Sawyer shows wisdom in innocence, courage in adversity and a marked sense of humour, all things which earn him our respect and force us to wonder whether we, as adults, are in fact superior.

Huck Finn

The character of Huck is established first by report. We are told that he is viewed by the adults of St Petersburg as a dangerous influence, free from the restrictions which are normally imposed on children and so likely to set a bad example to the other children. Tom, of course, envies Huck the freedom he has, but he also admires the boy. This admiration is shown to be well founded when, at the end of the novel, the figure of Huck comes into sharper focus. We see Huck showing courage in rushing to get help for the Widow Douglas and modesty in not wishing to receive any of the credit. He is a more pathetic character than Tom. Although he never feels sorry for himself, the adult reader sees a world of suffering in Huck's warning against women in Chapter 25: 'Tom, I reckon they're all alike. They'll all comb a body. Now you better think 'bout this awhile. I tell you better.' Obviously, Huck's mother has left him with a sorry impression of women and the idea that they all fight and drive men to drink.

Sympathy is also aroused when we hear Huck saying that he sleeps in barns and has to beg for food. He accepts this as the normal way of things, but to us it makes Huck seem a pathetic little boy. However, when Huck is taken into the fold, at the end of the book, and persuaded by Tom to accept the 'mothering' of the widow, we feel a twinge of regret: 'I'll stick to the widder till I rot, Tom; and if I git to be a reg'lar ripper of a robber, and everybody talking 'bout it, I reckon she'll be proud she snaked me in out of the wet.' Huck, the only truly free spirit in the book, is here prepared to enter the fold of civilisation and to substitute imagined for real adventure. As we see in the sequel to this novel, *Huckleberry Finn*, Huck does not find this brings him happiness and it is with relief that, at the end of it, we hear that he intends to 'light out' for still more unexplored territory, turning his back on civilisation in pursuit of freedom.

Huck shows most of the qualities possessed by Tom. He is, however, prepared to be led by the latter; it is Tom who knows what real adventure is, for he has read books. Huck's presence brings just a touch of sadness to the scene, for he has not got a secure base from which to go out into the world and he is forced to live on his wits in a way that Tom is not. If Tom's plans fail, then there is always Aunt Polly and a dry bed to return to; for Huck, there is no such solace. In the end, he gets the home and the bed, so is temporarily at least in as good a position as

Tom. Yet we doubt that this boy, who is so used to living for and by himself, will really fit into civilised existence. As he says, before being persuaded by Tom to stay with the widow, 'I won't be rich, and I won't live in them cussed smothery houses. I like the woods, and the river, and hogsheads, and I'll stick to 'em, too.' Huck is really much freer in spirit than Tom. He does not need to devote himself to escaping into the world of imagination in order to make life bearable, for real life, in the woods, is pleasant to him. He thus provides a contrast to Tom. One child is inventive because he needs to be, the other because he chooses to be. Needless to say, Tom can afford to be inventive, for his place in the world is secure and assured.

Becky Thatcher

Becky, unlike Tom and Huck, is a minor character, whose chief function is to act as inspiration for Tom; to be a pretty, defenceless little thing whom Tom can love and defend. As with all the other children, however, Twain has drawn Becky in a humorous yet telling way. She is prone to 'feminine' outbursts of tearful rage, she sulks, she follows her hero Tom around and then forces him to follow her, all things which adult females are liable to do when attempting to interest and capture a man's heart. She is, in other words, a miniature woman and a gentle parody of Woman.

Sid Sawyer

Sid is the complete opposite of his half-brother. He emerges as a rather dishonest little boy, willing to do anything in order to gain favour from adults, jealous of Tom and ever ready to get Tom into trouble. Sid lacks Tom's spirit and his intelligence is devoted to mean and despicable little acts, acts which may earn him the admiration of the adults but which lose him the sympathy of the reader. Indeed, Aunt Polly should, according to her own standards, prefer Sid to Tom, for Sid is obedient and likes church. But she is not without discernment, for she sees that Tom's spirit and inventiveness is preferable to Sid's faintly dishonest obedience.

Joe Harper

Joe also acts as a foil for Tom. He is one of those who need to be led, willing to join in Tom's games, but unable to initiate things himself. It is he who first weakens on Jackson's Island and wants to go home, thus giving Tom an opportunity to demonstrate his qualities as a leader of men.

Aunt Polly

Aunt Polly is an interesting character. She is very well-meaning, obviously loves her nephew Tom very much and spends her life in an agony of doubt, wondering why she should admire Tom when he thwarts her will so often and so well. In a sense, her simplicity allows Twain to show Tom's cleverness to better effect, but it also makes the reader aware that adults are more misguided than actually evil in what they do. Aunt Polly has nothing to offer except her great love for Tom, and this she does. But because she does love him, she wants him to grow up in a certain way and so tries to impose her will on him. She is such a pleasant character that the adult reader comes to like her and even, on occasion, to sympathise with her predicament in trying to tame her nephew. Yet she is, in the end, far less perceptive than Tom and so stands as one of the adults whose role in the book is to learn from youth. Twain does not condemn her. He merely shows that her failings are born of well-intentioned simplicity and that she has the greatest difficulty in reconciling her admiration for youth and liveliness with the sorts of repressions which society demands should be imposed on high-spirited children.

Mrs Thatcher and Mrs Harper

Mrs Thatcher and Mrs Harper act as foils for Aunt Polly. The women come together in their moments of grief, when they believe that their children are dead, and in these scenes their mutual helplessness is revealed. Mrs Harper, like Aunt Polly, is guilty of wrongfully accusing a child and so shares her feelings of self-reproach.

Mr Sprague, Judge Thatcher, the superintendent and the schoolmaster

It is significant that all the respectable male figures in the book should be remote from the children, working in a world of words which do not mean much, acting as forces which impose unpleasant tasks on the younger members of the community. Judge Thatcher is responsible for exposing Tom's ignorance in church, the schoolmaster seems to work by a system of punishments without any rewards and the two gentlemen connected with the church indirectly try to impose moral examples on the children. The remoteness of such figures allows the children greater freedom if, like Tom, they have little respect for what is remote and therefore irrelevant. The only men who seem to be intimately connected with the lives of the children are those such as Muff Potter and Jim, neither of whom can set the boys any example to follow but, instead, need care and protection from them.

Mr Jones

The old Welshman to whom Huck runs for help at the widow's house is respectable and makes contact with at least one of the children. He is, of course, a very minor character, but he shows the qualities of decisive action and paternal protection which are so rare in the book. His brief, understanding, and active presence serves to highlight what is missing from the world of the book in terms of masculine influence.

Muff Potter

Huck seems to understand Muff Potter better than anyone, for Muff is very like Huck's own father, continually in a drunken state. Muff is, of course, a weak character and a social outcast. Yet Tom and Huck have obviously had some dealings with him before the murder, showing once again that children do not discriminate on the same superficial grounds which adults use when rejecting someone. Muff is again a minor character, his chief function being to reveal the fundamental honesty and humanity of Tom. He does not emerge as a truly evil person, but rather as someone who is easily lead and quite helpless.

Injun Joe

Injun Joe is the one really evil character in the book. He does not just live outside the boundaries of civilisation, but he preys on that civilisation. He is, in fact, so evil and so lacking in any redeeming feature that he is almost a parody of a bad character. He certainly belongs to the pages of a boys' adventure story. But even with Joe, Twain lightens the tone of things at the end and allows him a splendid funeral, 'almost as satisfactory' to the townspeople 'as a hanging'!

Major points from the commentary

General

The novel is a humorous fantasy, written in the tradition of a boys' adventure story:

(1) It recreates the child's vision of the world.
(2) It entertains the adult by reminding him of his own childhood feelings and by showing him his own adult world from the viewpoint of a child.
(3) From this childish viewpoint, the adult world appears rather foolish.

(4) The few examples of narrative criticism of social institutions (education and the Church) are not made in a serious way.

(5) There is a distinct pattern of loss and gain throughout the novel. Tom's fortunes swing between the two and his moods follow suit.

Language

There are two distinct types of language, the narrative voice and the colloquial.

NARRATIVE:

(1) Twain makes fun of the characters by describing their activities in overly dignified terms.

(2) He also uses a broader and more obvious form of humour when dealing with the villagers and mankind in general.

COLLOQUIAL:

(1) The sound of the words is recreated through the spelling.

(2) The colloquial language is very vigorous.

Perspective

Twain uses the book to explore the perspective of the child and, by implication and through the use of the narrative perspective, to make gentle fun of the adult perspectives.

CHILDISH:

(1) Small sufferings are as hurtful to children as great sufferings to adults.

(2) Children are seen as comical in many of their actions and reactions.

(3) What the children do is modelled on adult activities, but with certain telling differences and even improvements, for example, they do not discriminate against people.

(4) The children are aware of the tedious or illogical nature of certain adult rituals, as, for example, church-going.

(5) Children use their imagination to escape boredom.

(6) Children seem to be able to cope extremely well with their own world and even succeed in teaching the adults some valuable lessons.

NARRATIVE:

(1) Twain sometimes puts the particular incidents in the book against a wider background of human folly.

(2) For the most part he seems to endorse the actions of the children, although he is amused by them.

(3) From time to time, he uses the narrative perspective to remind the reader that the heroes of the book are little boys.

Tom and literature

Tom enacts literary roles in his imaginary adventures, he himself is a miniature of many literary archetypes and, overall, he becomes a wholly new literary archetype.

LITERARY ROLES:
Tom's choice of literary figures, such as pirates, and so on, shows that his imagination is stirred by those *outside* ordinary society.

MINIATURE HERO:
(1) Tom looks faintly funny as, for example, a disappointed lover because he is so young.
(2) By using this little figure to fill out standard literary heroic poses, Twain makes these standard poses themselves look a little comical.

TOM AS ARCHETYPE:
Through the above, Twain creates a new literary archetype.

Characters

None of the characters is portrayed in any great depth. We penetrate some way into the mind of Tom, but that mind is itself fairly straightforward, experiencing joy and sorrow by turns as outside circumstances change. Tom is, of course, clever, and to some extent he dictates how the world will move. For example, he forces the whole town to suffer by deliberately disappearing and he largely dictates what Aunt Polly does. It is obvious that such control as he does exercise is aimed at making the world a more exciting or a more humane place, so we know that he has both imagination and humanity. His desire for a 'temporary ·death' is interesting from the psychological point of view. Tom is far too fond of life to want a permanent death, and this enthusiasm for living is his most outstanding characteristic.

Thus we see quite clearly Tom's psychological disposition, but that of the other characters matters far less. Their chief function is to act as a background for Tom, providing contrast, in the case of Huck, a following, in the case of Joe and Becky, an opportunity for real adventure, in the case of Muff Potter and Injun Joe. What these characters feel and think is scarcely relevant. What counts is how they impinge on Tom. So Twain draws them with broad strokes of the pen, providing a context in which his central character may operate. He also, by avoiding excessive concentration of people's feelings and thoughts, avoids the book becoming at all serious. Events have no serious or lasting repercussions for the characters, save Injun Joe and the doctor, so the whole story remains light and amusing, a pleasant, enjoyable book.

Part 4

Hints for study

Points for special study

The character of Tom Sawyer is obviously of central interest in this book, for it is Tom who initiates most of the actions in the book and it is his character which is portrayed in the greatest depth. Tom's youth, and the effects of this youth on his approach to the world, are worthy of attention. In trying to analyse the character of Tom Sawyer, the student might find the following questions useful:

(1) What sorts of things does Tom like doing? (for example, playing pirates)
(2) What sorts of things does he not like doing? (for example, going to church)
(3) How does he cope with unpleasant tasks? (for example, in the case of the fence-painting)
(4) What do Tom's likes, dislikes and ways of coping show us about his character?

Questions such as the above, which may be answered in a brief paragraph, will give the student a basic grasp of Tom's nature. More detailed insights will result from considering the following questions:

(5) How does Tom react when under stress? (for example, in court or in the caves)
(6) How does Tom react when he sees other people making mistakes? (for example, Aunt Polly and the medicine or Becky and the teacher's book)
(7) Do Tom's reactions under really distressing or threatening circumstances show us anything about his character?
(8) Does Tom have a moral code by which he runs his life?

By answering all these questions, the student should gain a firm idea of what Tom is like, how he goes about the world and what his approach to the world reveals about his character. One additional question might be considered, namely, 'Is Tom Sawyer an unconvincing character?' This question will lead the student into a consideration of the nature of the book as a whole. Tom is, perhaps, too good to be true, but is it necessary that he should be realistic when he is the hero of a humorous fantasy?

A second matter to consider in the book is the manner in which the narrator handles his material. The difference between the language of the characters and the language of the narrator has already been fully discussed under the heading of 'Language and style' and the student would be well advised to re-read that section before considering how Twain handles his material. The following questions should prove useful in an analysis of Twain's narrative method:

(1) How do we come to know the characters? (for example, in Chapter 1, does Twain tell us about the characters or does he let them speak for themselves?)
(2) At which points in the novel is the narrator most in evidence? (for example, Examination Evening, at church in Chapter 5, Chapter 33 and the conclusion)
(3) When the narrator is to the fore, what tone does he adopt and what point of view does he take on the events?
(4) How does the narrator regard his characters? (for example, Tom, Huck, Aunt Polly)
(5) Does the narrator have a personality of his own?
(6) What is the purpose of the book?
(7) Does the narrator succeed in his purpose?

The setting of the book is also of some interest. The student would be well advised to look at the way in which the town and the townspeople are described, how the river is used and how Jackson's Island and the haunted house are described. It is also a useful exercise to attempt to draw a little map of the town and its surroundings, all the places where important events take place and their respective positions. The map need not be very accurate in terms of distance, but the student will find this exercise of enormous help in enabling him to grasp the events and the topography of the book. Mark the salient event at each important spot, for example, the Temperance Tavern, the caves, the landing, Tom's house, Jackson's Island, and so on.

Once this exercise is completed, the student may then go on to consider what use Twain makes of the physical background. A few questions which might usefully be raised are:

(1) When does Tom take to the wilderness or the woods?
(2) What does he do there?
(3) How are these places described?
(4) What is the significance when, in Chapter 7, we see Tom gazing from the classroom out to the woods?
(5) Where does Tom feel most at home?
(6) Is the environment ever a threat to Tom?

These questions should lead the student to the interesting realisation that Tom's mood and the environment are bound up with each other, the mood being altered by the environment and the environment looking welcoming or threatening according to the mood of the character.

Study of characters other than Tom is also rewarding. In trying to discover how a certain character makes a certain impression on him, the student might consider the following questions:

(1) What role does the character play in the book in general terms? (for example, is it an adult or a child, in sympathy with Tom or opposed to him?)
(2) What sorts of things does the character say that indicate his/her preoccupations and outlook?
(3) What actions does the character perform which indicate the nature of that character? (for example, Injun Joe lies and commits murder)

Having decided on the nature of the character, the student might then like to give more detailed consideration to what role that character plays in relation to Tom, asking which aspects of Tom's personality are revealed through his connections with that character.

One of the most interesting aspects of the novel is the use which Twain makes of perspective. After re-reading the section dealing with this topic, the student should consider the following questions:

(1) In relation to any specific event, for example, the scene in court, from whose point of view is the event seen?
(2) Is the event seen only from one point of view or is there a combination of narrative and character perspective?
(3) What is the attitude of the reader to the event?
(4) What is responsible for creating this attitude?

After considering these matters, the student may care to go on to a more general analysis of Twain's use of perspective, exploring questions such as:

(5) How does the perspective of the child relate to the perspective of the adult characters?
(6) Whose point of view does Twain endorse, that of the child or that of the adult?
(7) What use does Twain make of the differences between the points of view of adult and child? (the student will first have to state what these differences are)
(8) In very general terms, what are the outstanding characteristics of the childish perspective?

The notion of perspective is the most complex one in the book, but the student who has worked his way through the questions on other topics should find that he has a sufficient grasp of the material to cope with this more complex matter. The student is reminded that all the questions posed in this section may be answered very briefly and, taken in groups, will give the skeletal framework of a more extended essay, which should, of course, include quotations to support the points being made.

Suitable quotations

The student may find that the following quotations are helpful in illustrating points that he may wish to make about the novel. Students should remember that when they include a quotation in an essay, they should state why they have included it, drawing attention to the implications of the quotation which they find of interest. The points which are illustrated by the quotations below are listed in brackets after the quotations themselves.

Chapter 1

'Like many other simple-hearted souls, it was her pet vanity to believe she was endowed with a talent for dark and mysterious diplomacy, and she loved to contemplate her most transparent devices as marvels of low cunning.' (Character of Aunt Polly/ the manner in which the narrator tells us about his characters)

'Not because his troubles were one whit less heavy and bitter to him than a man's are to a man, but because a new and powerful interest bore them down and drove them out of his mind for the time—just as men's misfortunes are forgotten in the excitement of new enterprises. This new interest was a valued novelty in whistling . . .' (Character of Tom/ pattern of loss and gain/ perspective of the child)

Chapter 2

'He had discovered a great law of human action, without knowing it— namely, that in order to make a man or a boy covet a thing, it is only necessary to make the thing difficult to attain.' (Nature of narrative humour/ character of narrator)

Chapter 3

'He wandered far from the accustomed haunts of boys, and sought desolate places that were in harmony with his spirit. A log raft in the river invited him, and he seated himself on its outer edge and contemplated the dreary vastness of the stream, wishing, the while, that he could only be drowned, all at once and unconsciously, without undergoing the uncomfortable routine devised by nature.' (Character of Tom/ pattern of loss and gain/ relationship between setting and mood/ child's perspective on suffering)

'Then her conscience reproached her [Aunt Polly], and she yearned to say something kind and loving; but she judged that this would be construed into a confession that she had been in the wrong, and discipline forbade that.' (Character of Aunt Polly/ the conflict felt by her between love for Tom and the need to discipline him/ the folly of adult reasoning, for Tom knows she is wrong)

'The window went up, a maidservant's discordant voice profaned the holy calm, and a deluge of water drenched the prone martyr's remains!' (Narrative humour)

Chapter 4

'He now looked exceedingly improved and uncomfortable. He was fully as uncomfortable as he looked; for there was a restraint about whole clothes and cleanliness that galled him.' (Tom's character/ effects of civilisation on children)

'Mr Walters was very earnest of mien, and very sincere and honest at heart; and he held sacred things and places in such reverence, and so separated them from worldly matters, that unconsciously to himself his Sunday-school voice had acquired a peculiar intonation which was wholly absent on weekdays.' (Narrative humour/ nature of adult rituals/ setting)

Chapter 5

'The minister gave out the hymn, and read it through with a relish, in a peculiar style which was much admired in that part of the country. His voice began on a medium key and climbed steadily up till it reached a certain point, where it bore with strong emphasis upon the topmost word and then plunged down as if from a springboard . . .' (Narrative humour/ adult folly/ language divorced from reality)

Chapter 6

'Huckleberry was cordially hated and dreaded by all the mothers of the town, because he was idle and lawless and vulgar and bad—and because all their children admired him so, and delighted in his forbidden society.' (Unkind attitude of adults to Huck/ perspective of children)

'Huckleberry came and went at his own free will. He slept on doorsteps in fine weather and in empty hogsheads in wet; he did not have to go to school or to church, or call any being master or obey anybody; . . . he never had to wash, nor put on clean clothes; he could swear wonderfully. In a word, everything that goes to make life precious, that boy had. So thought every harassed, hampered, respectable boy in St Petersburg.' (Nature of Huck Finn/ attitude of children to civilisation)

Chapter 8

'Now as to this girl. What had he done? Nothing. He had meant the best in the world and had been treated like a dog—like a very dog. She would be sorry some day—maybe when it was too late. Ah, if he could only die *temporarily* !' (Character of Tom/ pattern of loss and gain/ Tom as frustrated lover/ Tom's zest for life)

'The truth was, that a superstition of his had failed, here, which he and all his comrades had always looked upon as infallible. . . . Tom's whole structure of faith was shaken to its foundations.' (Role and importance of superstition)

Chapter 15

'He began to have a nobler opinion of himself than ever before. Still, he was sufficiently touched by his aunt's grief to long to rush out from under the bed and overwhelm her with joy—and the theatrical gorgeousness of the thing appealed strongly to his nature, too, but he resisted and lay still.' (Character of Tom)

Chapter 17

'As the service proceeded [the funeral service for the boys], the clergyman drew such pictures of the graces, the winning ways, and the rare promise of the lost lads, that every soul there, thinking he recognised these pictures, felt a pang in remembering that he had persistently blinded himself to them, always before, and had as persistently seen only faults and flaws in the poor boys. . . . The congregation became more and more moved, . . . till at last the whole company broke down and joined the weeping mourners in a chorus of anguished sobs, the preacher himself giving way to his feelings, and crying in the pulpit.' (Narrative humour at expense of town/ gullibility of adults/ language divorced from reality)

Chapter 21

'Vacation was approaching. The schoolmaster, always severe, grew severer and more exacting than ever, for he wanted the school to make a good showing on 'Examination' day . . . As the great day approached, all the tyranny that was in him came to the surface; he seemed to take a vindictive pleasure in punishing the least shortcomings. The consequence was, that the smaller boys spent their days in terror and suffering and their nights in plotting revenge.' (Unjustness of adults/ narrative perspective)

Chapter 24

'As usual, the fickle, unreasoning world took Muff Potter to its bosom and fondled him as lavishly as it had abused him before. But that sort of conduct is to the world's credit; therefore it is not well to find fault with it.' (Narrative perspective/ broad humour/ adult folly)

Chapter 35

'Huck Finn's wealth and the fact that he was now under the Widow Douglas' protection introduced him into society—no, dragged him into it, hurled him into it—and his sufferings were almost more than he could bear . . . whithersoever he turned, the bars and shackles of civilization shut him in and bound him hand and foot.' (Character of Huck/ nature of civilised society/ perspective of children/ narrative perspective)

Language

Students may find the language of the book difficult to understand at first. The difficulties arise because Twain wanted to recreate for his readers the idiom and the sound of the speech of the characters, so the book is full of apparently strange spellings and unfamiliar words. Most of the colloquial phrases can be understood either by studying the context in which they appear or by referring to the glossary following their first appearance. Students are advised to pay attention to the glossaries in order to familiarise themselves with the colloquial words and idiomatic expressions.

There are, however, certain patterns of spelling and certain words which occur very frequently. In order to assist the student in understanding the language of the book, these words and the 'odd' spellings are listed on the following page.

Words implying the threat of punishment:

to lam:	to beat, to hit
to lick:	to beat, to whip
to skin:	to flay, to whip
to tan:	to beat, to flay
to catch it:	to be punished

Abbreviated negatived verbs:

ain't:	am not or are not
warn't:	was not or were not
hain't:	have not
dasn't:	dare not

Common phonetic renderings:

becuz:	because
stiddy:	steady
kin:	can
bleeve:	believe
orter:	ought to
drownding:	drowning
shet:	shut
druther:	would rather
lemme:	let me
gimme:	give me
'pears:	appears
'tend:	attend
'spec:	expect
gwine:	is going to

Words in which 'ow' is spelt and spoken as 'er':

shadder:	shadow
swaller:	swallow
yaller:	yellow
foller:	follow
widder:	widow

Words in which 'th' is spelt and spoken as 'd':

dis:	this
wid:	with
dat's:	that is
furder:	further
murther:	murder

Words in which 'd' is spelt and spoken as 'e':

ole:	old
tole:	told

Sample questions and answers

In answering essay questions students should plan their answers so that the finished essay has an obvious structure. The planning may be undertaken with the help of additional subsidiary questions, a procedure illustrated in 'Points for special study' (pp.67–70). The opening paragraph of the essay should indicate briefly the areas with which the essay is going to deal and the closing paragraph should be a short statement of the student's overall argument. Statements in the essay should be backed up by reference to specific incidents or quotations.

---

(1) Discuss the character of Tom Sawyer.

The hero of *The Adventures of Tom Sawyer* is a likeable little boy with a great deal of vitality, imagination and resourcefulness. He is not, however, without faults, and can be rather rash, sometimes foolish and, on occasion, unkind. Mark Twain has carefully balanced the character of his hero so that he is never too good to be believable; indeed, the reader often finds himself admiring Tom in spite of his faults, not because of his virtues. As a character, Tom is used to allow the adult reader to re-enter the world of childhood and to rediscover the joys of living in a carefree way; he is also used to expose some of the follies in the adult way of ordering the world. Thus Tom is both someone whom the reader likes and admires and someone who is used to make a comment on the nature of the wider world, the world which adults and children share.

Tom's vitality and imagination are evident in almost everything he does. When the novel opens, Tom's Aunt Polly is calling for her nephew and this is a pattern which is repeated in various ways throughout the book. Tom is usually to be found somewhere other than where he is meant to be, doing something which gives him much more satisfaction than the tasks and rituals which adults try to impose on him. It is his love of life which leads him away from the school and into the woods, where he pretends to be Robin Hood. It is his love of life which makes him feel that the church is a boring place to be in and which enables him to find some enjoyment, even there, by concentrating on the movements of the dog rather than on the sermon. When the adult world becomes too much for Tom to bear, he simply leaves it and takes refuge either in the woods or on Jackson's Island. Even when he is very depressed, to the point of longing for death, Tom's love of life is so strong that he can only long for 'a temporary death'.

Tom's vitality, however, can lead him into trouble. When he goes into the caves with Becky, he is over-eager to explore the place and so he gets lost. Similarly, his imagination, which is usually useful to him in allowing him to escape from the dull realities of everyday life, can on occasion prove to be a liability rather than an asset. For example, it is Tom's vivid imagination which makes him suffer so much in the period between seeing Muff Potter in the cemetery with Injun Joe and the moment when he speaks out at the trial to clear Potter's name. During this period, he imagines all manner of horrible fates befalling him and he also imagines Muff Potter's plight in painful detail.

On the whole, however, Tom's imagination is very useful to him and its sheer force and scope lead the reader to admire him. When we see Tom completely absorbed in a game of 'pirates' or 'robbers', then we as adults are reminded of how vivid life seemed when we were children and how imagination provided an avenue of escape from care. As Twain says, 'Misfortunes are forgotten in the excitement of new enterprises' (Chapter 1). His imagination is also at the root of his resourcefulness. In the fence-painting scene, Tom uses his imagination in a very resourceful way and so not only avoids doing the tedious task himself but succeeds in making other boys pay to do it for him. In the caves, too, he shows that he is resourceful even when under great pressure. It is he who thinks of marking the path and he who eventually finds the way out. When dealing with his well-meaning Aunt Polly, Tom is very clever indeed. As she says on the first page of the book, 'I never did see the beat of that boy!', and this is a tribute to his resourcefulness. He always manages to outwit her. For example, when she is forcing him to take all sorts of patent medicines and unpleasant cures, Tom shows her the amount of suffering she is inflicting on him by giving the cat some of the medicine. In effect, he shows himself, both here and elsewhere in the book, to be rather more discerning than his aunt. The whole trip to Jackson's Island is designed to teach the adults of the village a lesson in how to treat children. Tom works it out that they will only appreciate himself and Joe when they think that they have lost them, and he is quite right.

However, Tom is not always right and when he returns from Jackson's Island his inventiveness and his imagination lead him to inflict real pain on poor Aunt Polly, who is quite convinced by his accurate 'dream', not realising that Tom was, in fact, in the room and witnessed the events of which he claims to have dreamt. When she rushes to tell her friends about this marvel, she soon learns the truth and is very upset indeed. Tom sees the folly of his ways and is ashamed of himself: 'His smartness of the morning had seemed to Tom a good joke before, and very ingenious. It merely looked mean and shabby now' (Chapter 19). This is Tom's only real unkindness, but elsewhere he is rash and foolish. His rashness lies at the root of his exposure in church, when his ignorance of the Bible proves that he had cheated in getting together the tickets which indicated he had a thorough knowledge of the book. It is foolish of him to claim that he is feeling ill, for he ought to know that Aunt Polly will take some action or other which will probably result in even greater discomfort than being in school, the fate which he is trying to avoid.

Indeed, it is fair to say that Tom is the creator of almost all the situations in which he shows his good and his bad qualities. For example, he is responsible for wandering too far into the caves, he is responsible for the boys being on Jackson's Island, and he is responsible for the trip to the haunted house. His questing and excitement-seeking attitude to the world leads him both into adventure and into trouble, and so gives him the opportunity to show what sort of child he is. On the whole, he is an admirable little fellow who gains our admiration and our sympathy. A great many of the things he does are inspired by a desire to escape from the world of the adults, the world of school, church and work, into the more exciting realms of the imagination. The world which Tom leaves behind him comes to seem, even to the adult reader, a far less attractive place than the world of childhood, and a no more sensible world than that of the child. Through Tom, Twain makes fun of the rituals and assumptions of the adult characters, mocking their reverence for formal education and showing us that Tom learns as much in the doing of things as in sitting in school. He also mocks the adult love of empty words, like those spoken by good schoolchildren and by the preacher. Such words have no bearing on reality, whereas Tom's imagined adventures often spill over into real life, where he becomes involved in finding buried treasure, exposing murderers and saving his lady-love. Thus Tom is a hero not only in his imagination but also in reality. Of course, Twain does to some extent exaggerate in the book. Tom's adventures are not all likely, but through them Twain is making two points. Firstly, he shows that where the character has a questing and exploratory attitude to life, he is likely to have a more exciting experience than the person who limits himself to a well-ordered and defined mode of existence. The latter sort of person is the adult, and the former is the child, so through Tom we see what the adult loses on his journey through life: some of the excitement, the vitality and the willingness to risk an upset in the normal routine. Secondly, Twain uses Tom's adventures to grip the imagination of his readers. The book is, in many ways, a typical adventure story for children and Tom fulfils his role as boy hero very well indeed, being both resourceful and brave.

While this second point is clearly necessary, since the book must entertain if it is to be read at all, the first point is more important and is what makes the book appeal to adult readers as well as to children. Tom Sawyer is a lively and likeable character whose role is both to entertain us and to reintroduce us to some of the lost joys of childhood, to the world where 'worthless' things like dead cats are treasured, where super-stitions are rife and cause great suspense, and where the imagination is a vital force in transforming everyday reality into something more attractive and more fulfilling. Tom Sawyer's zest for life is his most outstanding characteristic; this shapes his personality, making him reject many of the aspects of the adult world which seem to him to be against the love of life, making him feel sympathy for all other living things, from Muff and Huck to the insects, and making him into a quite remarkable child from whom adults may learn many lessons. He is both a character and possibly an appeal from Twain to his readers that they, too, should live life to the full.

---

(2) Discuss the nature of the humour in *The Adventures of Tom Sawyer*.

There are three levels of humour in *Tom Sawyer*. The first exists at the level of the characters' actions and experiences, the second lies in the disparity between these actions and experiences and the way in which they are described by the narrator, and the third is found in the more general comments made by the narrator about the world at large. All three levels are interwoven throughout the book to create an overall comic effect, but they are distinguishable from one another.

The first level of humour depends for its effect on our involvement with the characters. Once we have come to recognise Aunt Polly as a lovable, well-meaning, but fairly simple woman, then we will find her battles with her nephew Tom amusing. We like both Aunt Polly and Tom, once we get to know them; and when they are engaged in a struggle over something or other, we can laugh at Tom's manoeuvrings and Aunt Polly's reactions. For example, in Chapter 12, Tom gives the cat some of the medicine with which his aunt has been treating him. The effect on the cat is startling; the animal dashes all round the room and eventually disappears out of the window. This spectacle is humorous in itself, but the dialogue which ensues between Tom and Aunt Polly is even more amusing. 'Now, sir, what did you want to treat that poor dumb beast so, for?', asks Aunt Polly, to which Tom replies, 'I done it out of pity for him—because he hadn't any aunt.' Aunt Polly immedi-ately falls into this trap by saying, 'Hadn't any aunt!—you numbskull. What has that got to do with it?' This gives Tom the chance to teach her a lesson by making her see that her well-meant treatments are, in fact, tortures. 'Heaps,' he replies. 'Because if he'd a had one she'd a burnt him out herself! She'd a roasted his bowels out of him 'thout any more feeling than if he was a human!' The humour in this exchange depends on our knowledge of the two characters involved; we derive satisfaction and amusement from seeing both of them operating in their usual ways,

Tom being cunning and rather clever, Aunt Polly being simple and completely at his mercy. Interchanges between the characters all work on this level, being humorous because of the events themselves and because of the personalities involved.

The second level of humour is also evident in Chapter 12. We see the actions and experiences of the characters being described by the narrator in a very high-flown, 'literary' way which is comically inappropriate to the situation. In an attempt to put an end to all the various treatments, Tom claims to be very fond of a particularly nasty medicine called 'Painkiller'. His aunt is, of course, suspicious of this sudden passion and her feelings are described as follows: 'If it had been Sid, she would have had no misgivings to alloy her delight; but since it was Tom, she watched the bottle clandestinely. She found that the medicine really did diminish, but it did not occur to her that the boy was mending the health of a crack in the sitting room floor with it.' From what we know of Aunt Polly and Tom, this suspicious attitude to Tom is well warranted. The narrator chooses to describe this suspicion in language which is remote from the kind of language which Aunt Polly herself would use; words such as 'clandestinely' are beyond the scope of her vocabulary and are also out of all proportion to what is actually going on. This word is used to comic effect simply because it is so dignified, and its dignity contrasts sharply with the reality being described, namely, watching the amount of medicine in a bottle. Twain is gently mocking his own characters by using this technique; the reader sees that the word is out of proportion to the actual events, and he also sees that the lack of proportion reflects something of Aunt Polly's attitude to the affair. She no doubt feels rather secretive and cunning in watching the bottle in this way, having an inflated idea of the importance of what she is doing.

The first level of humour, that generated by the actions and experiences of the characters and communicated by their exchanges, and the second level, where the words of the narrator mirror the exaggerated importance attached to trivial events by the characters, are often put into a wider perspective of more general human folly. Chapter 12, for instance, contains an example of this humorous technique. At the outset of the chapter, Twain tells us that Tom is unhappy and that his aunt is worried. He then gives the reader the background to the kind of action which Aunt Polly decides to take:

> She began to try all manner of remedies on him. She was one of those people who are infatuated with patent medicines and all newfangled methods of producing health or mending it. She was an inveterate experimenter in these things. When something fresh in this line came out she was in a fever, right away, to try it; not on herself, for she was

never ailing, but on anybody else that came handy. She was a subscriber for all the 'Health' periodicals and phrenological frauds; and the solemn ignorance they were inflated with was breath to her nostrils . . . and she never observed that her health journals of the current month customarily upset everything they had recommended the month before.

The above quotation not only gives us a gentle mockery of Aunt Polly's attachment to amateurish medicine; it is also a fairly detailed attack on the whole amateur medicine business, which was a very profitable one in America at the time when the book was written. Although Twain is very funny about the medicine and those who believe in it, he is also making a serious point, perhaps hoping to dissuade real-life 'Aunt Pollys' from attempting every false cure that might come their way. Thus, the third level of humour extends beyond the book itself and out into the real world. It is satire, mockery by exaggeration, and has the traditional aim of all good satire, namely, to destroy or undermine the phenomenon which is being mocked.

It is obvious that the book contains these three levels of humour and that they are carefully interwoven. In this single chapter, we find examples of all three and each fits quite naturally with the others. When Twain uses humour of the third kind, the reader is not aware that he is being preached at, for the 'sermon' is directed at him through the medium of the characters. These characters are funny in themselves. None of them has any great psychological depth and they might all be described as 'types' rather than individuals. For instance, Aunt Polly is a fairly standard model, the doting and well-meaning older woman who is having to cope with children who are not her own, and Tom is the adventurous and clever little boy hero. Each character comes from a fairly standard literary mould. What is original and humorous is Twain's grouping of these standard figures, their interrelationships, such as the battle of wits between Aunt Polly and Tom, and the kinds of situations into which they are put. Thus the book contains three levels of humour and a group of characters used in a humorous way, the whole thing being made comic and enjoyable by Twain's adroit use of language and the pace at which he makes the book move.

---

(3) Discuss how Mark Twain portrays and uses the child's view of the world in *The Adventures of Tom Sawyer*.

The child's view of the world is central to *The Adventures of Tom Sawyer*, for the hero of the book is a child. Mark Twain shows us young characters who, because they are physically small and are as yet not fully integrated into adult society, see the world from a different angle to the adults and have different priorities and values from them. The children do not know the 'rules' according to which the world works, so they make up their own rules, substituting barter for money and superstition for religion. They also make much greater use of their imagination than any adult, escaping into a world of adventure and excitement whenever the real world seems at all tedious.

The physical smallness of the children has a number of side effects. In the first instance, they are much nearer the ground than the taller adults, and so they take a keener interest in the things which crawl on the ground, such as the insects. We see Tom swapping his tooth for a tick, taking a great interest in a pinch bug when in church and, on Jackson's Island, noticing with a keen eye the movements of a little worm: 'The marvel of Nature shaking off sleep and going to work unfolded itself to the musing boy. A little green worm came crawling over a dewy leaf... Now a procession of ants appeared, from nowhere ... A brown-spotted ladybug climbed the dizzy height of a grass blade ... A tumblebug came next, heaving sturdily at its ball, and Tom touched the creature ...'. This matter of perspective is made explicit later in the book, when, in Chapter 22, Tom feels threatened by a thunderstorm: 'It might have seemed to him a waste of... ammunition to kill a bug with a battery of artillery, but there seemed nothing incongruous about the getting up such an expensive thunderstorm as this to knock the turf from under an insect like himself.' This makes plain the connection between the children, the insects and the adults. Just as the children watch the world of the insects, so the adults watch the world of the children, with interest but without much understanding, and neither insects nor children are aware of their comparative insignificance. It is the narrator of the book who creates this awareness of relative size in the reader and shows just how significant size is in dictating the perspective, or view of the world, of the children. They are small, the world is large, and the disparity between the two can be either a cause of excitement, as, for example, when Tom wanders 'away from the haunts of men' and into the realms of the imagination, or a source of terror, as on Jackson's Island during the storm or in the seemingly endless caves.

Twain also shows the reader that the children see the world as being arranged in a certain way which differs from the adult view of its organisation. Where the adults use money as the mode of exchange, a commonly agreed substance, of indisputable value, the children do not have money. They deal much more directly, exchanging things rather than money and establishing, in any given set of circumstances, the relative values of different objects. When Tom persuades his fellows that fence-painting is a highly desirable occupation which is worth paying for, the payments take the form of pieces of broken glass, half-eaten apples, a kitten with one eye, a dead cat, a dog collar with no dog, and so on. On the strength of these items, Tom feels that he is 'literally rolling in wealth'. This is an accurate piece of observation on Twain's part; children do tend to treasure things which adults regard as useless. Their set of values is quite different from that of the adults, taking no account of the usefulness of any object but relying on their own personal liking for a thing. In this way, Twain reminds the adult reader that things do not have any intrinsic value, although the adult world seems to assume they have. Children work at the basic level, where value depends entirely on personal need or preference, and so they have a much more direct and much simpler relationship with worldly goods.

This simplicity of evaluation is also apparent in the attitude of the livelier children to such institutions as the church or school. Those children like Sid, who only want to impress the adults, pretend to like going to church or to school. The more honest children, who judge things by their own standards, find both places tedious on the whole. Tom is bored by the sermon in church and the reader can see that his boredom is justified, for the sermon has nothing whatsoever to do with the kinds of experience he is likely to have in St Petersburg; references to Oriental despots seem, both to Tom and to the reader, to be quite irrelevant. The adult characters see them as being justified, for they feel that they are privileged to live in a democracy and smugly pity those who are subject to tyranny. However, as Tom knows only too well, life in America is not democratic. Someone is always telling him to do something and he has very little say in what happens to him. Once again, Twain uses the simple insights of the children to throw doubt on the kinds of assumptions which underlie the adult world and, once again, it is the view of the children which comes nearer to the actuality of the situation.

In one area the children are not closer to reality. Where the adults seem to believe that the world is organised by God, who works out a system of rewards and punishments, the children tend to see God as fairly remote. They pin their faith on more immediate phenomena, working out their fates according to superstitions. This belief in superstition is very deep. When Tom finds that burying a marble does not cause the marble to multiply, we are told: 'But now, this thing had actually and unquestionably failed. Tom's whole structure of faith was shaken to its foundations' (Chapter 8). Superstitious beliefs about warts lead Tom and Huck to the graveyard on the night of the murder and superstitious beliefs about stray dogs cause them a moment of awful panic afterwards, when one of these harbingers of death appears to be coming in their direction. The significance of superstition is that, like almost all other childish notions, it brings immediate gratification or disappointment. The children are not prepared to wait a long time for their rewards and punishments; they expect them to occur within a very short space of time. This is not unreasonable, for it is true that, when Tom does something wrong, the punishment follows shortly after. Through superstition, this notion of immediate, rather than delayed, results following on actions is fitted into a wider context; given the added dimension of the supernatural, or metaphysical, it becomes the child's version of religion. It is perfectly possible that Twain meant the adult reader to question whether his own religious beliefs have any more solid or sensible a foundation than the superstitious beliefs of the children. Certainly, orthodox religion, as he portrays it, is a senseless ritual, accompanied by many restrictions on freedom and by the minister and superintendent using special and silly voices. Twain accurately observes that children are prone to superstitious belief; he not only shows the reader this but uses this system of belief as a means of raising a question about the adult system.

Twain also portrays the children as having a far greater capacity than the adults to use imagination. Whilst the adults are trapped with their 'reality', obeying the Church and following respectable paths, the children are free to roam at will through the pages of literature and through the woods, identifying with, and acting the parts of, legendary heroes and heroines. The imagination is, at least for Tom, a place where he can escape from the impositions of the adult world, a place where he can be his own master or any kind of person he wants to be. Twain shows us that this escape route works very well indeed, allowing the children to come to terms, very rapidly, with unhappiness or disappointment. 'Within two minutes, or even less, he had forgotten all his troubles. Not because his troubles were one whit less heavy and bitter to him than a man's are to a man, but because a new and powerful interest bore them down and drove them out of his mind for the time' (Chapter 1). Imagination not only takes the form of playing roles. It also enables Tom to find original and effective ways of coping with reality, as in the fence-painting episode; here it is his inspired imagination which leads Tom to acquire his great wealth and to avoid the tedious task. Once again, Twain shows us that his adult characters are much more rigid than the children. Where they work along predictable and acceptable lines, using money, going to church, doing their duty and generally behaving as they feel they are expected to behave, the children are much more flexible, aware of how they are meant to behave but refusing very often to do so. Their minds and spirits are much freer and the adult reader is once more left to wonder about the sorts of restrictions which he accepts as being necessary in life.

Thus Twain portrays the child's view of the world as one which is much simpler, more imaginative and less restricted than the outlook of the adult. He has accurately observed the ways in which children think and operate, using everything, from their physical smallness to their vivid imagination, to lend conviction to his portrait of the world of childhood. He then gently contrasts the views of the children with the views of the adults and leaves his readers with some implicit questions about their own concepts of reality and respectability and how far these mirror actual needs and feelings. Huck Finn's comment on the world of the Widow Douglas may well echo the sort of thing which Twain, through his portrayal of the child's vision of the world, is saying to his adult readers, 'The widder eats by a bell; she goes to bed by a bell; she gits up by a bell—everything's so awful reg'lar a body can't stand it.'

---

(4) Is *The Adventures of Tom Sawyer* simply a book for children, or does it offer the adult reader some satisfaction?

It was only in response to the insistence of his wife and of his fellow writer, W.D. Howells, that Mark Twain agreed to say that *Tom Sawyer* had been written for children. He himself had originally wished to say, in his preface to the book, that it was for adults. Certainly, the book would appear, on the surface, to be very much a book for children. It has as the main character and hero a little boy, it deals with adventures, both imaginary and real, and it does not seem to have any great depth. Twain's idea that it was a novel for adults must have been based on two features of the book, its ability to remind the adult of what it was like to be a child and its implicit questioning of the adult way of ordering the world. It succeeds very well in achieving these two aims, but it is also a novel which does appeal to children because it is a book about children and gives the child reader the chance to identify with its characters.

If we look at the surface level of the book, the level on which it does appeal to the younger reader, then we see that it resembles in many ways the 'boys' adventure story'. Such stories were not restricted by ideas of what was likely or probable. They ranged freely through a series of adventures and coincidences unlikely in real life. The stories also had little boys as the heroes, boys who showed outstanding courage, resourcefulness and imagination. Tom Sawyer fits into this literary mould very well indeed. He is courageous in standing up in court to clear the name of Muff Potter, he is courageous in the caves when he tries to keep Becky's spirits up and he is courageous when he is faced with the threat of punishment in school. His resourcefulness is apparent in almost all that he does, be it avoiding painting a fence or keeping the other two boys on Jackson's Island until the time for returning to the village has arrived. Tom's imagination, too, is always at the ready. He uses it when he is playing games such as Robin Hood, he relies on it when he is searching for buried treasure, he needs it to sustain him through the tedium of sitting in church, listening to a boring sermon. In every way, Tom is just the sort of character who would appeal to children. They would admire his courage, resourcefulness and imagination, identify with him in his running battle with adult authority and feel for him when he is misunderstood by adults or thwarted in love.

On this surface level, Tom is a lively enough character and no doubt the adult reader can derive a measure of enjoyment from reading about his adventures and his experiences. This, however, is not sufficient to sustain the interest of the adult, far less to make the book one which was written specifically for him. Whilst the actual adventures may be what inspire the child reader, the adult reader is more interested in the memories which Tom's outlook on the world inspire and in the attitudes to the world which Tom holds.

For the adult reader, *Tom Sawyer* is a vivid evocation of what it feels like to be a child. Mark Twain accurately analysed and recreated these feelings in the book, and in doing so, reminded his readers of the days when they, too, were children. He lays some stress on the size of the children; their small physical stature has many repercussions, not least of which is that they are liable to take an interest in things even smaller than themselves, such as insects and worms. When Tom wakens on Jackson's Island, we have the following almost lyrical evocation of this childish interest:

> Gradually the cool dim gray of the morning whitened, and as gradually sounds multiplied and life manifested itself. The marvel of Nature shaking off sleep and going to work unfolded itself to the musing boy. . . . A brown-spotted ladybug climbed the dizzy heights of a grass blade, and Tom bent down close to it and said, 'Ladybug, ladybug, fly away home, your house is on fire, your children's alone,' and she took wing and went off to see about it—which did not surprise the boy, for he knew of old that this insect was credulous about conflagrations, and he had practiced upon its simplicity more than once. A tumblebug came next, heaving sturdily at its ball, and Tom touched the creature, to see it shut its legs against its body and pretend to be dead. The birds were fairly rioting by this time. A catbird, the northern mocker, lit in a tree over Tom's head, and trilled out her imitations of her neighbors in a rapture of enjoyment . . .
> (Chapter 14)

The satisfactions in this passage for the adult reader are many. Firstly, it does remind him of the simple, unselfconscious outlook of childhood, the total absorption in tiny things which is so much a feature of our youthful life. Tom is as one with Nature in the above passage, integrated into the scene by the little insects which crawl over and around him. It is an idyllic image of childish innocence and enjoyment and, as such, serves to remind the reader of the state of mind which went with such innocence.

Secondly, the passage has a certain ironic undertone; the adult reader can see a parallel between Tom, overseeing the little world of the insects without really understanding it, and the adults, who oversee the world of the children in an equally uncomprehending way. Throughout the book, Twain allows us to enter the world of the children, and from that angle it is clear to us that the adult characters do not really understand at all what is going on in that world. There is one major difference, however. Tom does not try to alter the world of the insects, he is simply an interested observer; but the adults do try to alter the world of the children, attempting to make it resemble their own in shape. The adult reader who is aware of this parallel also becomes aware of a strain of implicit criticism of adult assumptions.

Apart from emphasising the size of the children and their capacity for complete union with the world of Nature, Twain also reminds the adult of the days when things which now seem to be of no value were regarded as treasures. The children are, of course, faintly comic, in their attachment to such unlikely and useless things as dead cats, but they are also a touching reminder of days when things were not judged on the basis of their usefulness, merely on the grounds of their immediate appeal to any would-be possessor. Here again the adult reader is reminded of his former self and, if he is alive to ironic undertones, he will also see that Twain is implicitly questioning adult assumptions about the value of things. Money, when looked at in this light, is merely worthless and usually unattractive paper, no better really than a dead cat! This dual strain of reminiscence and implicit criticism is apparent in many of the topics dealt with in the book. Superstition and religion are implicitly compared, the ritual of going to church is brought into question, the rationality of patriotic utterances is cast into doubt and generally most of the practices, rituals and assumptions of the adult reader are brought into question by being compared with the practices, rituals and assumptions of the childish world. Twain not only takes his adult reader on a nostalgic journey back into childhood; he also poses questions about where exactly the adult has reached in moving away from childhood.

This level of implicit criticism, together with the nostalgic re-creation of a more innocent state of being, is the chief recommendation of the book to the adult reader. Nor is the criticism always simply implicit. Occasionally Twain makes it more explicit, although retaining the light, humorous tone which runs through the book as a whole. After all difficulties have been resolved and Tom and Huck have got hold of the treasure, we are told:

Wherever Tom and Huck appeared they were courted, admired, stared at. The boys were not able to remember that their remarks had possessed weight before; but now their sayings were treasured and repeated; everything they did seemed somehow to be regarded as remarkable; they had evidently lost the power of doing and saying commonplace things; moreover, their past history was raked up and discovered to bear marks of conspicuous originality. The village paper published biographical sketches of the boys. (Chapter 35)

This is fairly blatant mockery of the world and the values of the adult characters in the book and also a gentle mockery of the values which the adult readers themselves may hold in everyday life. The alteration in the estimation of the boys has been brought about entirely because of their newly acquired wealth and Twain is obviously pointing out how arbitrary and unstable the adult powers of discrimination are, for the boys are receiving adulation and admiration out of all proportion to their real worth, which has not altered at all in the course of the book. They have not changed as people; they have merely got hold of a lot of money. In passages such as this Twain's desire to question the assumptions of the adult world emerges most clearly; but this desire is implicit in almost every incident in the book, and it is this level of criticism which may well have made him wish to claim initially that the book was only for adults. Instead, he succeeded in writing something which appeals to both adults and children, something which is both humorous and relatively profound.

Part 5

Suggestions for further reading

The text

The Adventures of Tom Sawyer, Signet Classic, New American Library, New York, 1979

Modern editions of other works by Mark Twain

The Adventures of Huckleberry Finn, Penguin Books, Harmondsworth, 1970
A Connecticut Yankee in King Arthur's Court, edited by Justin Kaplan, Penguin Books, Harmondsworth, 1971
The Innocents Abroad, Signet Classic, New American Library, New York, 1966
Life on the Mississippi, Signet Classic, New American Library, New York, 1966
Roughing It, Signet Classic, New American Library, New York, 1979
Pudd'nhead Wilson, Penguin Books, Harmondsworth, 1969
Tom Sawyer Abroad and *Tom Sawyer Detective*, Macmillan, London, 1962

General critical writings on Mark Twain

BROOKS, VAN WYCK: *The Ordeal of Mark Twain*, Dutton, New York, 1920. An argument that Twain's genius was impeded by his American background
COX, JAMES: *Mark Twain, The Face of Humor*, Princeton University Press, New Jersey, 1966. A well-argued and penetrating study of Twain as a humorist
DE VOTO, BERNARD: *Mark Twain at Work*, Harvard University Press, Cambridge, Mass., 1963. An answer to Van Wyck Brooks, arguing convincingly that Twain was inspired, and not impeded, by his background
GRANT, DOUGLAS: *Twain*, Oliver & Boyd, London & Edinburgh, 1962. A general introduction
KAPLAN, JUSTIN: *Mr Clemens and Mark Twain*, Cape, London, 1967. A useful factual study of Twain's life

LYNN, KENNETH S.: *Mark Twain and Southwestern Humor*, Little, Brown and Company, Boston, 1959. A perceptive study of the comic tradition and Twain's work

SMITH, HENRY NASH: *Mark Twain: The Development of a Writer*, Harvard University Press, Cambridge, Mass., 1962. A readable study of technique in Twain's work

SMITH, HENRY NASH (ED.): *Mark Twain: A Collection of Critical Essays*, Prentice-Hall, New Jersey, 1963. A useful collection of criticism

The author of these notes

MARY ROSS is a graduate of the University of Stirling (BA, PhD); she holds a Secondary School Teaching Certificate and a Diploma in Education from the University of Dundee. She is Head of the English Department at Newbattle Abbey, an Adult Residential College at Dalkeith, near Edinburgh. She is at present completing a critical study of William Faulkner.

The first 100 titles

CHINUA ACHEBE	*Arrow of God* *Things Fall Apart*
JANE AUSTEN	*Northanger Abbey* *Pride and Prejudice* *Sense and Sensibility*
ROBERT BOLT	*A Man For All Seasons*
CHARLOTTE BRONTË	*Jane Eyre*
EMILY BRONTË	*Wuthering Heights*
ALBERT CAMUS	*L'Etranger* (*The Outsider*)
GEOFFREY CHAUCER	*Prologue to the Canterbury Tales* *The Franklin's Tale* *The Knight's Tale* *The Nun's Priest's Tale* *The Pardoner's Tale*
SIR ARTHUR CONAN DOYLE	*The Hound of the Baskervilles*
JOSEPH CONRAD	*Nostromo*
DANIEL DEFOE	*Robinson Crusoe*
CHARLES DICKENS	*David Copperfield* *Great Expectations*
GEORGE ELIOT	*Adam Bede* *Silas Marner* *The Mill on the Floss*
T.S. ELIOT	*The Waste Land*
WILLIAM FAULKNER	*As I Lay Dying*
F. SCOTT FITZGERALD	*The Great Gatsby*
E.M. FORSTER	*A Passage to India*
ATHOL FUGARD	*Selected Plays*

MRS GASKELL	*North and South*
WILLIAM GOLDING	*Lord of the Flies*
OLIVER GOLDSMITH	*The Vicar of Wakefield*
THOMAS HARDY	*Jude the Obscure* *Tess of the D'Urbervilles* *The Mayor of Casterbridge* *The Return of the Native* *The Trumpet Major*
L.P. HARTLEY	*The Go-Between*
ERNEST HEMINGWAY	*For Whom the Bell Tolls* *The Old Man and the Sea*
ANTHONY HOPE	*The Prisoner of Zenda*
RICHARD HUGHES	*A High Wind in Jamaica*
THOMAS HUGHES	*Tom Brown's Schooldays*
HENRIK IBSEN	*A Doll's House*
HENRY JAMES	*The Turn of the Screw*
BEN JONSON	*The Alchemist* *Volpone*
D.H. LAWRENCE	*Sons and Lovers* *The Rainbow*
HARPER LEE	*To Kill a Mocking-Bird*
SOMERSET MAUGHAM	*Selected Short Stories*
HERMAN MELVILLE	*Billy Budd* *Moby Dick*
ARTHUR MILLER	*Death of a Salesman* *The Crucible*
JOHN MILTON	*Paradise Lost I & II*
SEAN O'CASEY	*Juno and the Paycock*
GEORGE ORWELL	*Animal Farm* *Nineteen Eighty-four*
JOHN OSBORNE	*Look Back in Anger*
HAROLD PINTER	*The Birthday Party*
J.D. SALINGER	*The Catcher in the Rye*

SIR WALTER SCOTT	*Ivanhoe* *Quentin Durward*
WILLIAM SHAKESPEARE	*A Midsummer Night's Dream* *Antony and Cleopatra* *Coriolanus* *Cymbeline* *Hamlet* *Henry IV Part I* *Henry V* *Julius Caesar* *King Lear* *Macbeth* *Measure for Measure* *Othello* *Richard II* *Romeo and Juliet* *The Merchant of Venice* *The Tempest* *The Winter's Tale* *Troilus and Cressida* *Twelfth Night*
GEORGE BERNARD SHAW	*Androcles and the Lion* *Arms and the Man* *Caesar and Cleopatra* *Pygmalion*
RICHARD BRINSLEY SHERIDAN	*The School for Scandal*
JOHN STEINBECK	*Of Mice and Men* *The Grapes of Wrath* *The Pearl*
ROBERT LOUIS STEVENSON	*Kidnapped* *Treasure Island*
JONATHAN SWIFT	*Gulliver's Travels*
W.M. THACKERAY	*Vanity Fair*
MARK TWAIN	*Huckleberry Finn* *Tom Sawyer*
VOLTAIRE	*Candide*
H.G. WELLS	*The History of Mr Polly* *The Invisible Man* *The War of the Worlds*
OSCAR WILDE	*The Importance of Being Earnest*